The Parables of Grace

by
Robert Farrar Capon

WILLIAM B. EERDMANS PUBLISHING COMPANY
GRAND RAPIDS, MICHIGAN

Copyright © 1988 by Wm. B. Eerdmans Publishing Co.
255 Jefferson Ave. S.E., Grand Rapids, Mich. 49503

Library of Congress Cataloging-in-Publication Data:

Capon, Robert Farrar.
    The parables of grace.

    1. Jesus Christ—Parables.   I. Title.
BT375.2.C3216 1988   226'.806   88-3737

ISBN 0-8028-3648-8

.

Contents

CHAPTER ONE   Introduction:
A Parable of Theology and Faith   1

CHAPTER TWO   Death and Resurrection:
The Touchstone of the Parables of
Grace   7

CHAPTER THREE   The First Parable of Grace:
The Coin in the Fish's Mouth   19

CHAPTER FOUR   Losing as the Mechanism of Grace:
The Lost Sheep   31

CHAPTER FIVE   Death, Resurrection, and Forgiveness:
The Unforgiving Servant   40

CHAPTER SIX   Losing as Winning:
The Prologue to the Good Samaritan   51

CHAPTER SEVEN   The First of the Misnamed Parables:
The Good Samaritan   58

CHAPTER EIGHT   Grace More Than Judgment:
From the Friend at Midnight to the Rich
Fool   68

CHAPTER NINE   Fruitfulness out of Death:
The Watchful Servants and the Barren
Fig Tree   84

CHAPTER TEN   Interlude on an Objection:
Why Not Life Rather Than Death?   99

CHAPTER ELEVEN   Back to Death, Lastness, and Lostness:
The Mustard Seed, the Yeast, and the
Narrow Door   104

CONTENTS

CHAPTER TWELVE   Death and the Party:
The Transition to the Great Banquet
    117

CHAPTER THIRTEEN   The Party Parables:
The Great Banquet and the Prodigal
Son   129

CHAPTER FOURTEEN   The Hardest Parable:
The Unjust Steward   145

CHAPTER FIFTEEN   Death and Faith:
Lazarus and Dives   152

CHAPTER SIXTEEN   The Scandal of the Gospel:
The Returning Servant, the Ten Lepers,
and the Vultures   160

CHAPTER SEVENTEEN   God as Anti-hero:
The Unjust Judge   171

CHAPTER EIGHTEEN   Death and Resurrection One Last Time:
The Pharisee and the Publican   178

CHAPTER ONE

Introduction

A Parable of Theology and Faith

I know it is a risky thing to begin a book on Jesus' parables of grace with a parable of my own on the perils of theologizing; nevertheless . . .

A certain couple once built a house. They set it on solid foundations and made it proof against all weathers. But in their haste to take up occupancy, they made no provision for access to the front door. To enter, they simply leaped up onto the doorsill and yanked themselves in. As they began to feel more at home, however, they decided to make their comings and goings more convenient. First, they built a short flight of steps. These served well for a while, but eventually they replaced them with a small, plainish porch on which they could sit and contemplate the excellences of their house. In good weather, they even entertained friends there with wine, cheese, and conversation.

Soon enough, though, they tore down this first porch and built a much larger one. They gave it a roof supported by carpenter gothic columns; they surrounded it with intricate railings; they provided it with a wide, low-pitched staircase; and they decorated it everywhere with gingerbread ornamentation.

Many years passed, during which they enjoyed both the porch and the house. But then, on a cold and stormy night, the woman came to the man as he sat by the fire and shook a sheaf of bills in front of him. "Have you ever considered," she said annoyedly, "how much we spend on the upkeep of our porch? For something that's usable only four months of the year—and not even then, if one of us is sick—the cost-benefit ratio is appalling. Between the dry rot and the peeling paint, not to mention the lawsuit your friend Arthur brought against us when he caught his ankle in the gap left by those missing boards, it's more trouble than it's worth. Tear it down and let's go back to the way we started: no porch, no steps, no nothing; just up into the house by one leap."

My parable, obviously, is about the relationship between faith and theologizing. Equally obviously, it is more an allegory than a parable; but since even Jesus allowed himself a number of such simple, this-stands-for-that stories, let it pass. My point in starting with it is to put what I am up to in this book into perspective. The house in which the couple lived represents faith—the simple act of deciding to trust Jesus (and, consequently, Jesus' words as we have them), no matter what we, on any given day or in any given intellectual weather, may happen to think about them. On the other hand, the various accesses, plain steps or fancy porches, that they added to their house stand for our attempts at theologizing—that is, for any and all of the explanations we come up with when we try to render our house of faith more intelligible, more attractive, or more acceptable to the intellectual tastes of our neighbors or friends.

Inevitably, any author who tries to interpret Jesus' parables will spend most of his time on the porch. He will, of course, take it for granted that there is a house of faith to which the porch should remain firmly attached, and he will, if he is wise, make it clear that only the house can provide a completely safe place in which to live. Nevertheless, since the woman in my parable came to such a dim view of porches, a few comments on her objections would seem to be in order.

It is tempting simply to agree with her. So much of what both the world and the church consider to be the essential message of the Gospel is simply interpretation. It is generally assumed that Christianity teaches that people cannot be saved unless they accept some correct, or at least some Official Boy Scout, understanding of what Jesus did or said. Take the atonement, for example—the scriptural insistence that our sins are forgiven by trusting a Jesus who died on the cross and rose from the dead. The usual view is that this trust inevitably involves accepting some intellectual formulation of *how* Jesus' death and resurrection could possibly have achieved such a happy issue out of all our afflictions. You know: he was able to bring it off because he was both God and man and so could bridge the gulf that sin had put between the two; or, his death was effective because it was a ransom paid to the devil; or, it did the job because the power of his sacrificial example softened even hard hearts and moved people to better behavior; or, his resurrection solved the problem of sin because it brought about a new creation in which sin had no place. The point is not whether any of those interpretations is true, or even adequate (some are more so, some less); it is that none of them is strictly necessary for laying hold of the atonement Jesus offers. All you need for that is to believe in *him*—to say "Yes, Jesus, I trust you," as opposed to "No, Jesus, get lost." Your subsequent understanding of how such a simple yes can do so vast a work may make you glad, sad, scared, or mad; but in no case can it be what saves you—or, for that matter, condemns you.

This distinction needs to be applied just as much to the words of Jesus as it does to his works. People tend to think that unless they can arrive at some satisfying interpretation of this parable or that, the parable in question may safely be left out of account. But just as the work of Jesus (say, in his death and resurrection) has whatever effect it has quite independently of the theologies we happen to hammer onto it, so Jesus' words—simply because they are Jesus himself speaking—have whatever power he has, no matter what we may think about them. His parables are not so much word-pictures about assorted external subjects as they are *icons* of himself. Like good poems, they not only *mean,* but *be:* they have a *sacramental* effectiveness. Whether we "get" them or not, therefore, they remain first and foremost his way of *getting to us.* They are lights shining out of the house of faith itself, inviting us home. What we do with them as we sit out on the porch of interpretation may make us appreciate them more or less, but it cannot damage the lights, and it certainly doesn't turn them off.

As an instance of how all this applies in practice, consider how it corrects a misconception of what we commonly call the teaching of the faith. Christian education is not the communication of correct views about what the various works and words of Jesus might *mean;* rather it is the stocking of the imagination with the icons of those works and words themselves. It is most successfully accomplished, therefore, not by catechisms that purport to produce understanding but by stories that hang the icons, understood or not, on the walls of the mind. We do not include the parable of the Prodigal Son, for example, because we understand it, nor do we omit the parable of the Unjust Steward because we can't make head or tail of it. Rather, we commit both to the Christian memory because that's the way Jesus seems to want the inside of his believers' heads decorated. Indeed, the only really mischievous thing anyone can do with the Gospel is insist on hanging only the pictures he happens to like. That's what heresy really is: picking and choosing, on the basis of *my* interpretations, between the icons provided to me. Orthodoxy, if it's understood correctly, is simply the constant displaying of the entire collection.

Still, interpretation, like porch-building, is practically inevitable. We are, after all, *thinking* beings, and we think about everything we do, up to and including the act of faith: almost no one lives out an entire lifetime simply by leaping into the ungarnished doorway of the house of faith. Accordingly, the woman in my parable was advocating a rather more austere lifestyle than most of us are in fact willing to put up with. Let's see, then—assuming that her husband took exception to her comprehensive demolition plans—what might be said for his more tolerant view of the situation.

No doubt he would begin by conceding her valid points: first, that a porch is no place to live; second, that porch-builders often betray a taste for the rococo; and last, that porches rot faster than houses. The work of theological interpretation has the same drawbacks. To begin with, it is mostly just a fun thing to do in good company on a warm afternoon when your kidney stones are not acting up. If it is taken much more seriously than that—if it is seen as the center from which life derives its meaning—it will fail us in precise proportion to our need to make it succeed. In all of us, there are doubts and despairs (to paraphrase Auden) smoldering at the base of the brain; everyone who rests his life on his ability to hold his world together by an intellectual synthesis runs the risk that someday, years hence perhaps, the doubts will suddenly "blow it up with one appalling laugh."

Likewise, theological thought has a penchant for elaborating itself beyond not only sense but good taste. Once someone devises a system or theme for building the porch to his faith, the temptation is to continue the work of construction whether it serves the purposes of the house or not. Hence all the theologies that manage to take the Gospel of grace—of forgiveness freely offered to everyone on the basis of no works at all—and convert it into the bad news of a religion that offers salvation only to the well-behaved. Hence, too, all the moralistic interpretations of the parables: sermons on the duty of contentment from the Laborers in the Vineyard, and little lessons in loveliness from the parable of the Good Samaritan.

Finally, all systems of theological interpretation, plain or fancy, rot out at an alarming rate. Unlike the house of faith, they are exposed to the wind and weather of prevailing opinion. Even if a theologian never once doubts anything about his system, it remains endlessly vulnerable to scorn, ridicule, or just plain disinterest from the outside. The sheer labor of keeping up with the repairs necessitated by such forces has kept more theologians than one from ever spending as much as a single night under a snug roof.

Still, having made those concessions, the man in my parable would insist that porch-building, whether it is inevitable, worthwhile, tasteful, expensive, or not, is a fact. Most people who have faith have some intellectual structure tacked in front of it. But precisely because that is true, those who invite others to visit or to stay in their house of faith are faced with a difficulty: *the only way to get guests to the door is to walk them across the porch.* Theologizing may not be a saving proposition, but it lies between almost everybody and the Saving Proposition Himself.

Accordingly, he would point out that there is something to be said, no matter how much or how little porch you have on your faith, for keeping that structure as attractive and sound as you can. Its uprights should be set solidly on concrete Gospel footings. Its stringers—the principal interpretative devices by which the flooring is held up—should be made of something scripturally sound, not of humanistic balsa wood or used timbers from someone's old, collapsed theological building. Above all, its floorboards must be all in place and all nailed down tight. It will not do for anyone to leave spaces in the decking—to install only the scriptural boards he likes and to omit those he doesn't. A theological porch must include every side of every scriptural paradox. A system, for example, that is all love and no wrath is no better than one that is all wrath and no love. In either case, the unsuspecting guest is liable to break an ankle because of what was left out.

But enough. My parable was as much, or more, for me as for you. If you will try not to insist that my porch be exactly like yours, I shall resist the temptation to force mine on you. All I really care about is that both our structures have no missing boards. So for now, come up on my porch and have a seat. Here begins the work of interpreting the parables.

CHAPTER TWO

Death and Resurrection

The Touchstone of the Parables of Grace

On the principle that the simplest plan is the best, I propose to deal with the parables of Jesus in the order in which they occur in the Gospels of Matthew, Mark, and Luke. Naturally, this requires that the discrepancies in these accounts—their sometimes differing sequences of events and materials—be harmonized into a single order; but rather than invent a harmony of my own, I shall take the liberty of adopting the numbering system for Gospel passages devised by Kurt Aland in the Greek-English edition of the *Synopsis Quattuor Evangeliorum* (United Bible Societies).* Beyond that, there are only a few other housekeeping details to be noted. I shall be working from the original Greek, principally from the text employed by Aland in the *Synopsis* but also from the second edition of the Aland, Black, Martini, Metzger, Wikgren text, from the twenty-second edition of the Nestle text, and from the Schmoller Concordance. The translations offered will be largely my own, but they will take into account the versions I habitually consult, namely, the King James Version (KJV), the Revised Standard Version (RSV), Today's English Version (TEV), the New International Version (NIV), and, to a lesser degree, the Clementine Vulgate (VgCL), the Jerusalem Bible (JB), the New English Bible (NEB), and the New Testament in Modern English by J. B. Phillips (JBP).

Looking at Jesus' parables as a whole, I find that they can be divided into three consecutive groups. The first group consists of

---

*An English edition of *Synopsis of the Four Gospels* is available from the American Bible Society for $8.95. It is the ideal companion to this book for study purposes.

what I call the parables of the kingdom, namely, the parables that occur in the Gospels prior to the feeding of the five thousand (that is, before Matt. 14, Mark 6, and Luke 9). I have already dealt with these elsewhere.** The second group, which I shall call the parables of grace, includes all the parables, acted as well as spoken, that the Gospel writers place between the feeding of the five thousand and the triumphal entry into Jerusalem (the latter occurring at Matt. 21, Mark 11, and Luke 19). The final group, the parables of judgment, consists of the remaining parables, almost all of which the Gospel writers place between the triumphal entry and the beginning of the passion narrative (at Matt. 26, Mark 14, and Luke 22).

While all such divisions are to some degree arbitrary, it seems to me that this one has the merit of relating Jesus' parables to the development of his thought about the nature of his messianic mission. Consider, for example, my choice of the feeding of the five thousand as the point of transition from the parables of the kingdom to the parables of grace.

At the beginning of his ministry, Jesus presents himself as a fairly standard-issue messianic claimant. He exorcises demons, he gives sight to the blind, he makes the lame walk, he heals lepers, he restores hearing to the deaf, he raises the dead, and he proclaims good news to the poor. Not only that, but he teaches as one having authority in himself, and not as the scribes and Pharisees. In short, he appears as the kind of wonder-working rabbi to whom at least the common people flock enthusiastically. Even at this early stage, however, he also indulges in certain un-messianic actions that inevitably upset the religious authorities of the day. He breaks the sabbath, he associates with tax collectors and prostitutes, and, in general, he sits conspicuously loose to the law-abiding expectations that the Jewish establishment had for any proper Messiah. Indeed, even before he presents his parables of the kingdom, the Pharisees and the Herodians have already begun to think about killing him (Matt. 12, Mark 3, Luke 6).

Still, there is an element in his thinking—namely, the centrality to his mission of his own death and resurrection—that has not yet been clearly formulated. True enough, the early kingdom parables (especially those that employ the imagery of seed being put into the

**See *The Parables of the Kingdom* (Grand Rapids: Zondervan, 1985).

ground) are not incapable of being given a death-resurrection interpretation; but in telling them, Jesus does not yet seem to be talking about his own dying and rising. These early parables focus chiefly on the paradoxical *characteristics* of the kingdom; they portray it as catholic rather than parochial, actually present rather than coming at some future date, hidden and mysterious rather than visible and plausible; and they set forth the bizarre notion that the responses the kingdom calls for in the midst of a hostile world can vary from total involvement to doing nothing at all. But these first parables do not, in any developed way, enunciate the paradoxical *program* by which the kingdom is in fact accomplished, that is, by death and resurrection.

The development of that theme comes, as I see it, only in the parables of grace—and it comes after a series of events and utterances (Aland nos. 144-164) that show Jesus more and more preoccupied with death. Beginning with the death of John the Baptist (Matt. 14, Mark 6; cf. Luke 3), and continuing through the feeding of the five thousand (Matt. 14, Mark 6, Luke 9, John 6), the first prediction of his death and resurrection (Matt. 16, Mark 8, Luke 9), the transfiguration (Matt. 17, Mark 9, Luke 9), and the second prediction of his death and resurrection (Matt. 17, Mark 9, Luke 9), he gradually reaches a clear realization that the working of the kingdom is mysteriously but inseparably bound up with what Luke (9:31) calls his "exodus"—in other words, with the passion and exaltation that he is shortly to accomplish in Jerusalem.

Accordingly, I plan to argue that just as this line of thinking was bound to become manifest in Jesus' actions from those events onward, so too it informed his mind as he developed his parables of grace. True enough, some of those parables do not seem immediately susceptible of a death-resurrection reading. Still, since many of them have such an interpretation written plainly on their face—and since even some of the more obscure of them are remarkably patient of it—I propose to interpret as many of them as possible under that rubric. I am aware of the dangers of trying to turn a single notion into the master key to an admittedly diverse collection of materials; but since death-resurrection becomes, from this juncture in the Gospels onward, the overmastering notion in Jesus' mind, I propose at least to try it in every possible parabolic lock. Where it does not fit, I shall cheerfully give up on it; in all honesty, though, I do not anticipate having to exercise such stoic cheer too often.

One slight digression to meet an objection sometimes voiced by biblical critics. It is often said that Jesus himself (Jesus as he actually lived and thought as opposed to the Jesus presented to us by the writers of the Gospels) could not possibly have seen his ministry in death-resurrection terms—that such categories were the handi-work of the community of faith that succeeded him and that they are far too "churchy" for attribution to anyone in Jesus' circumstances. I do not know about that, nor do I think the critics know either. As far as I am concerned, the Jesus of the Gospels is the only available Jesus there is and it is idle to postulate any other, no matter how likely such a Jesus may seem on the grounds of form criticism or historical surmise. For my money, it was over the literary presentation of this Jesus of the Gospels that the Holy Spirit brooded when inspiring the Scriptures; the same cannot be said for subsequent literary ef-forts on Jesus' behalf. If the presentation we accept by trusting biblical inspiration is in error, then not only are we stuck with it; we will never even (on any basis, "inspired" or "factual") be able to say exactly what it is in error about.

I go, therefore, directly to the record as we have it. In Matthew, the account of the death of John the Baptist (Matt. 14:3-12; Aland no. 144) is put into narrative almost immediately after the comple-tion of the parables of the kingdom. In Mark (at 6:17-29), it comes after only a handful of other events (Jesus stills a storm, exorcizes the Gerasene demoniac, raises Jairus's daughter, and commissions the Twelve—Aland nos. 136-142). Moreover, both Gospel writers in-troduce the death of John with the statement that Herod the te-trarch, on hearing about Jesus' reputation, took the view that Jesus was John the Baptist risen from the dead (Matt. 14:1-2; Mark 6:14-16; Aland no. 143; cf. Luke 9:7-9).

It strikes me that we do not make enough of the occurrence of John's death in this early stage of Jesus' ministry. To begin with, the identification of Jesus as the risen Baptizer (not only by Herod, but by a good many others) could easily have had the effect of making Jesus wonder about the relationship of his mission to that of John. He could well have asked himself whether his messiahship would continue to stress the plausible, interventionist kind of program that John proclaimed, or whether it would turn out to be something far more mysterious, indirect, and paradoxical—all of which notions, it should be observed, he had already developed to a considerable extent in his parables of the kingdom.

Fascinatingly, even before John was killed, Jesus had begun to make distinctions between himself and his cousin. When John heard in prison about the works of the Christ (Matt. 11:2), he sent his disciples to ask Jesus if he was "the coming one." Jesus initially replies almost as if John is a superior who deserves a full report. He gives the messengers a reassuring list of his actions: the blind receive their sight, the lame walk, lepers are cleansed, the deaf hear, the dead are raised, and the poor have the good news preached to them. But then he adds, perhaps sensing that John may nevertheless find his style too bizarre, "happy is he who is not scandalized by me" (Matt. 11:5-6). In any case, the messengers leave and Jesus addresses himself to the crowds. John, he tells them, is not just a prophet; he is much more than a prophet. In fact, he is the forerunner of Jesus himself and thus is greater than anyone who ever lived. Still, Jesus goes on, anyone who is even the least in the kingdom of heaven is greater than John (Matt. 11:7-11).

Then, however, Jesus delivers a comment in which he begins to develop the distinction between himself and John. Admittedly, the passage in question (Matt. 11:12-15) can be taken simply as an extension of what he has already said about John: but I am disposed to make something more of it. "From the days of John the Baptist until now," Jesus says, "the kingdom of heaven suffers violence and the violent seize it by force. All the prophets and the law up to John prophesied; and if you want to accept it, John is Elijah whose coming was predicted. If you have ears, listen." It seems to me that even at this early juncture (the passage precedes even the parables of the kingdom in Matt. 13), Jesus is groping to differentiate his ministry from John's. John and the prophets, he says, proclaimed a kingdom that would be brought about by plausible exercises of force—by what might be called direct, or straight-line, or right-handed power. Jesus does not say here, in so many words, that his own style of exercising power will be indirect, paradoxical, and left-handed; but in the parables of the kingdom he is about to unfold, he will depict a kingdom that works in a veritable snowstorm of mystery, indirection, and implausibility. Not only that, but just before beginning those parables (on the occasion of the scribes' and Pharisees' asking him for a sign: Matt. 12:38-42), he says that no sign will be given to this evil and adulterous generation except the sign of Jonah—which he then goes on to identify as a reference to the death and resurrection of the Son of man. It is at least possible, therefore, to hold that even before the account of the death of John the Baptist in Matt. 14, Jesus is portrayed as putting some intellectual distance between his mission and John's. It also seems fairly likely that, in Jesus' mind, the defining principle of that distance will ultimately have some important connection with death.

We can only surmise, of course, how much intellectual contact Jesus had with John through his formative years. Even though they were cousins, it is probably unwise to make merely putative closeness the basis for either agreement or disagreement between them. From the Gospel records we have, however, it seems clear that Jesus, while he may have started out in a vein like John's, gradually came to see his cousin as the proclaimer of a less paradoxical kingdom than the mysterious one he found himself delineating. In any case, by the time Jesus finally arrived at the point of his own death, his distancing of himself from John's approach was profound and absolute. I feel free, therefore, to hold that from John's death onward, Jesus found himself progressively more liberated from whatever ties he may still have had to the non-paradoxical style of kingdom proclamation. His last link to the old order was gone; he could now get on with the new.

The way is open, accordingly, to see the events that come next in the sequence (the feeding of the five thousand, the predictions of his death and resurrection, the transfiguration) as perhaps the greatest single crux in Jesus' human thinking about his mission. To take generalities first, consider the obvious fact that the tone of Jesus' ministry changes radically after the transfiguration. From that point on, the messianic claimant who began his career as a wonder-working rabbi does fewer and fewer "miracles" and indulges in far less purely "ethical" discourse. More than that, the largely "upbeat" style of his earlier ministry is replaced by a "setting of his face toward Jerusalem"—that is, toward his coming death and resurrection.

But there is harder evidence. Consider the feeding of the five thousand. After a long day in a deserted spot—a day in which Jesus preoccupied himself with the old-style work of healing and teaching that had marked his ministry so far—the disciples come to him and suggest dismissing the crowd so the people can go and get something to eat. At first, Jesus seems hardly to have heard them: "You feed them," he says. It is only after they have nattered on about the cost of such a project that Jesus even begins to concern himself with the problem. With an air of grudging involvement (John's Gospel, admittedly, does not support this), he says, "Go see how much bread you have." Even then, though, his concern manifests itself in an almost minimal way. He simply takes the five loaves and two fish, gives thanks, and proceeds to have the disciples pass them out. The "miracle" is about as understated as it can possibly be: Jesus, from start to finish, seems largely "out of it." Not only that, but when the miracle is over and everyone has finally caught on to what has happened, it looks for all the world as if he cannot get away from the scene soon enough.

He dismisses both the disciples and the crowd (the four accounts differ slightly about the details at this point) and goes up on the mountain all by himself. John's Gospel actually gives the reason for this retreat: Jesus knew they were going to come and seize him *in order to make him king* (John 6:15). Even without that assertion, however, the other accounts are susceptible of the same interpretation: Jesus seems to be having second thoughts about the style of his ministry so far and he goes off by himself to wrestle with these doubts in prayer. And pray he does—for most of the night, in fact. Then, in a scene that has a dreamlike quality, he comes walking to his disciples on the water. The usual interpretation of this scene is that he was coming to their aid in a storm; but Mark (6:48) says that "he was going to pass them by"—suggesting once again that Jesus was less involved in their problems than in his own. In any event, the disciples end up more afraid of Jesus (despite his airy "Cheer up, it's me; don't be afraid") than they were of the storm. The impression given by the account is that something darkly mysterious was preoccupying not just his mind but his entire being. The disciples seem to have been responding more to that mystery than to the sudden calming of the storm: they were, as Mark says (6:51-52), "completely amazed and utterly confused, because they did not understand about the loaves, and their hearts were hardened."

Obviously, it is possible to interpret this last comment as meaning that, having failed to grasp the first "miracle," they likewise missed the second. Possible, but hardly likely. They had already seen

Jesus do enough signs and wonders to keep them, presumably, from that kind of egregious point-missing. No, their incomprehension was caused not by their inability to know a miracle when they saw one but by an unfathomable scariness emanating straight from Jesus himself. He was being *weird*. He was, for all his visibility, off their mental radar screens.

In a fascinating way this weirdness is underscored in the Fourth Gospel by the discourse (John 6:22-71) that follows the feeding and the walking on the water. The next day, as John has it, the crowd finally catches up with Jesus at Capernaum on the other side of the lake. They, too, are puzzled—specifically by the fact that Jesus seems to have made the crossing without using the only available boat. "Rabbi," they ask, "when did you get here?" Jesus' response simply adds to their confusion: he first launches into a petulant comment on the unworthiness of their motives in seeking him; then, in reply to their plausible, even sincere, questions, he indulges himself in a series of progressively more obscure answers.

What they really want, as John has already noted, is to make him king; but they also hope that he will claim for himself the kind of kingship they have in mind. Accordingly, having just witnessed the "sign" he has done in feeding the five thousand, they begin asking him "bread from heaven" questions designed to elicit the desired response from him. "Our fathers ate manna in the desert," they say (6:31), obviously expecting that he will pick up on the lead and come out with a punch line characterizing his messiahship as an updated version of the kind of plausible, interventionist salvation they know and love.

But Jesus gives them naught for their comfort. He tells them not only that Moses didn't give them bread from heaven but that the true bread from heaven is the one who comes down from heaven and gives life to the world. The rest of the dialogue proceeds in the same way: they ask sensible, leading questions and Jesus gives weird, non-responsive answers. He promises resurrection at the last day (6:39, 40, 54); he reaffirms that *he* is the living bread from heaven and then adds that the bread he will give is his flesh (6:51); and he ends with the assertion that unless they eat his flesh and drink his blood, they cannot have life in themselves (6:53). Finally, not only the crowd but also many of Jesus' disciples simply go away and no longer walk with him (6:66). In short, by his references to flesh and blood, he has broached the subject of the death of the Messiah—and the weirdness of it all has simply put them off. Even the twelve, who do in fact remain with him, stay on only in a dumb and desperate, "to whom can we go?" kind of way.

I am aware that many critics are unwilling to admit the testimony of John's Gospel into the kind of argument I am making. I have no such reluctance. It seems to me that however this material came to be included in the Fourth Gospel, it is still very much of a piece with the weirdness already present in Matthew, Mark, and Luke up to this point, as well as with the weirdness yet to come in their accounts of the remaining events prior to the parables of grace. For if the synoptic Gospels have not yet plainly set death at the center of Jesus' strangeness at this time, they have nevertheless carefully laid the foundation for proclaiming its centrality. Not only that, but they will shortly, in their accounts of Peter's confession and of the transfiguration, set it forth in just so many words. Accordingly, I find that what John's Gospel presents in chapter 6 agrees nicely with what the other three give in the parallel passages, and I make no apologies for arguing from it.

But to continue. Look next at Peter's confession (Matt. 16, Mark 8, Luke 9) and note how it brings together all the elements I have been expounding so far: Jesus' relationship to John the Baptist; his unique messiahship; and his bizarre linking of that messiahship to his own death and resurrection. The passage begins with Jesus' asking his disciples whom people say he is. They answer, John the Baptist—or Elijah, or one of the prophets. In other words, they tell Jesus that he is being taken for someone who is part of the old, plausible, non-paradoxical order of things. Jesus then asks them whom *they* say he is, and Peter answers, the Christ. But Jesus rebukes them (I am following Mark at this point, 8:30), telling them not to talk to anyone about him. Presumably, he does this to preclude their broadcasting their own old-style, non-paradoxical notions of messiahship; and he follows it up by predicting, in plain words, his coming death and resurrection. Peter, in turn (proving that Jesus was right not to trust his disciples' understanding of messiahship), rebukes Jesus (as Matthew has it, Peter simply cannot stand hearing such "down" talk from someone he's just proclaimed Messiah). Finally, Jesus once again rebukes Peter ("Get behind me Satan . . ."), telling him he's out of step with God's way of doing the messianic business at hand. The whole exchange, as far as I am concerned, produces exactly the same reading on the "weirdness scale" as did the dialogue in John 6. It shows Jesus as a paradoxical dying-and-rising Messiah who fits no previous mold, and it continues to stress the off-putting strangeness he has been manifesting all through this sequence.

Which brings us to the capstone of the entire series of events, the transfiguration of Jesus (Matt. 17, Mark 9, Luke 9). Except for the resurrection itself, it is the single strangest event in his ministry; and it sets together once again the theme of old-order-versus-new and the theme of death as the key to Jesus' messiahship. The first of these is evidenced by three details: it is Moses and Elijah (old-order figures) who speak with Jesus; Peter suggests building three tents— indicating that he could think of no way to commemorate the event other than with a ritual from the old religion; and God, apparently out of sheer impatience with the disciples' failure to grasp the new order in Jesus, simply drops a cloud on the lot of them and tells them to pay attention to his beloved Son. The theme of death is manifested not only by Luke's already-mentioned reference (9:31) to the topic of the conversation among Jesus, Moses, and Elijah (namely, his "exodus"), but by Mark's report (9:9) that Jesus ordered the disciples to tell no one what they had seen until the Son of man had been *raised from the dead*.

The transfiguration, accordingly, brings us to the end of my argument for placing the paradox of Jesus' death at the center of his thinking as he approaches the first of his parables of grace, that is, the parable of the Lost Sheep. Before moving on, though, it is worth noting the precise passages that intervene here. The transfiguration (Matt. 17, Mark 9, Luke 9) stands at Aland no. 161, and the Lost Sheep (Matt. 18, Luke 15) at no. 169. Let me simply list the materials that nos. 162-168 comprise. They are: the disciples' question about the "second coming" of Elijah (Matt. 17:10-13; Mark 9:11-13; no. 162); the healing of a boy with an unclean spirit (Matt. 17:14-21; Mark 9:14-29; Luke 9:37-43a; no. 163); Jesus' second prediction of his death and resurrection (Matt. 17:22-23; Mark 9:30-32; Luke 9:43b-45; no. 164); the miracle of the coin in the fish's mouth (Matt. 17:24-27; no. 165); the disciples' argument about who is the greatest (Matt. 18:1-5; Mark 9:33-37; Luke 9:46-48; no. 166); the comments about the freelance exorcist

(Matt. 10:42; Mark 9:38-41; Luke 9:49-50; no. 167); and the warnings against giving scandal by failing to appreciate the bizarre demands of Jesus' paradoxical ministry (Matt. 18:6-9; Mark 9:42-50; Luke 17:1-2 and 14:34-35; no. 168). Of these, only three need comment here. (A fourth, the coin in the fish's mouth, is actually an acted parable and thus deserves separate treatment as a prologue to the parables of grace.)

Jesus' second prediction of his death and resurrection (Aland no. 164) stands, obviously, as yet another nail hammered into the already solid structure of mysterious messiahship that he has been building before the disciples' eyes. But it is not the only such nail driven home here. When the disciples argue about who is greatest (no. 166), Jesus tells them that anyone who wants to be first must be last of all and servant of all. He then stands a little child in their midst and puts his arms around him, saying, "Whoever receives one such little child in my name receives me."

We twentieth-century Christians—with our basically nine-teenth-century view of childhood as a wonderful and desirable state—miss the point of this passage. In Jesus' time, and for most of the centuries since, childhood was almost always seen as a less than human condition that was to be beaten out of children as soon as possible. Therefore when Jesus sets up a little child as an example, he is setting up not a winsome specimen of all that is simple and charming but rather *one of life's losers*. He is telling his disciples that if they follow him in his mysterious messiahship, they will—like him—have to become something no one has any real use or respect for. He is exalting not the plausible greatness that is the only thing the world understands but the implausible greatness that he himself intends to pursue. He is, in short, proclaiming his own version of what Paul in 1 Cor. 1 later set forth as the "foolishness of the preaching," namely, that God works not in the great, the wise, and the powerful but in the weak and the foolish: "for the foolishness of God is wiser than men and the weakness of God is stronger than men" (1 Cor. 1:25).

Accordingly, even though Jesus' holding up of the little child contains no reference to death as such, I find that his emphasis here on life's "little deaths"—his exaltation of a panoply of unsuccesses which, before he is done, he will round out to include lastness, leastness, and lostness, as well as littleness and death itself—is part and parcel of his ever-deepening awareness of himself as a Messiah who will do his work not at the top of the heap, as everyone expects, but in the very depths of the human condition. Likewise, I find that Jesus' warnings (no. 168) against scandalizing "one of these little ones" have the same force. His disciples are to be extreme in their pursuit of lastness, lostness, and littleness: "If your hand scandalizes you, cut it off . . ." (Mark 9:43ff.). They are to become, in other words, what he will become: despised and rejected. Only at that extremity, Jesus insists, can anything saving be done about the world.

With that much as stage-setting, therefore—and with a paradoxical Messiah now standing in the wings fully cognizant of death and resurrection as the modus operandi of his saving work—we are finally ready to hear, perhaps with newly opened ears, his parables of grace.

CHAPTER THREE

The First Parable of Grace

The Coin in the Fish's Mouth

I find it intriguing that the first of the parables of grace—the coin in the fish's mouth—is acted out rather than told as a story. While this is not an uncommon technique for Jesus to use (into the category of acted parables I put not only this episode but also his temptation in the wilderness, his walking on the water, his casting of the money-changers out of the temple, his cursing of the fig tree, and above all, his resurrection and ascension), it is a method that has given many biblical critics acute discomfort. Since actions like the ones cited have in them a generous helping of the frankly mysterious or the gratuitously spectacular, critical minds are sometimes tempted to dismiss them as inauthentic—as fabrications by later and lesser writers bent chiefly on miracle-mongering.

The coin in the fish's mouth, for example, strikes such critics as far too close in tone to the miracles attributed to Jesus in the so-called apocryphal Gospels. Confronted with the spectacle of Jesus' telling Peter he will find money for a tax payment in the first fish he pulls up out of the sea, they can only take it as an instance of theological larking around. They find it more akin to the spurious stories in which the boy Jesus makes clay animals and birds come to life than to what they consider his more "serious" or "worthy" miracles of compassionate healing. And even if they do not dismiss the story completely, their consternation at it leads them to view it as a mere "floating fragment," a piece of scriptural jetsam that a canonical Gospel writer (Matthew alone, in this case) has moored at 17:24-27 for lack of any better notion of where to put it.

There are two things wrong with that approach. First, the apocryphal Gospels are not *mere* fabrications: on any fair view, they are extrapolations of authentic traditions made by writers who felt that extra doses of the miraculous were just the thing to bring the picture of Jesus more into line with their particular theological predilections. In other words, they took genuine, if minor, elements in the orthodox tradition and created additional and more bizarre instances of them. Jesus, in the canonical Scriptures, does in fact do a number of things that cannot easily be fitted into anyone's theological system. It is questionable procedure, however, to dismiss such peculiarities simply because they do not come up to some critic's idea of scratch.

Take, for example, the parables in general. While it is fair to say that almost all of them are light-years away from being mere allegories—and while it is equally just to issue warnings to preachers that they should avoid allegorical interpretations of major parables like the Prodigal Son or the Laborers in the Vineyard—it is definitely not cricket to hold that when we find Jesus making an allegory out of one of his own parables (as in his interpretations of the Sower and of the Wheat and the Weeds) we must conclude that such allegorizing is not the work of Jesus but of some later hand. Likewise, it is just as much of a mistake to dismiss the apparently frivolous miracle of the coin in the fish's mouth. At the very least, we should make every attempt to give it an interpretation—even if it turns out to be a wildly unusual one—that takes seriously and *in context* the admitted unusualness of the act itself.

Indeed, it is precisely this failure to take difficult passages in context that is the second thing wrong with the dismissive approach. To decide in advance that the coin in the fish's mouth has been parked where it is just because Matthew, or somebody, felt obliged to preserve something he did not understand is to fly in the face of both common sense and biblical inspiration. It violates common sense because Matthew (I have no interest in arguing whether the evangelist was a he, a she, or a they) was obviously closer to the event itself, or at least to witnesses of the event, than were any subsequent commentators. Not only that, but he was clearly no slouch at putting together Gospel materials (his work did, after all, beat out the apocryphal competition). At the very least, we should begin our efforts at commentary by assuming he had sound reasons for every particular placement of his pericopes, and we should be slow to decide he didn't.

In addition, the dismissive approach runs counter to a serious attempt to do justice to biblical inspiration. For even if Matthew did in fact end up inserting the episode of the coin in the fish's mouth at 17:24 out of sheer desperation, there was still (as far as Christians are concerned) Somebody Else brooding over Matthew's work—a sovereign Somebody, if you please, who could use even mindless insertion to get the material where he wanted it. I have in mind, of course, the Holy Spirit, the ultimate presiding genius of Scripture— for whom indirection is as good as direction, which in turn is as good as verbal dictation—and who was not above using any or all of those devices when, where, and as he saw fit. Once you believe *that*—once you hold that by the inspiration of the Spirit, "the Holy Scriptures of the Old and New Testaments are the Word of God and contain all things necessary to salvation," it seems fairly reasonable to assume that the Spirit got not only the words but their placements right. Accordingly, it is also appropriate to bend over backward if necessary in your efforts to figure out just what he might have had in mind. Context, therefore—whether of Matthew's devising or of the Spirit's—will govern my consideration of the coin in the fish's mouth from start to finish.

To begin, though, let me simply set down the story itself, noting some problems of translation as I go. Matthew 17 contains the following materials: the transfiguration (17:1-13), the healing of a boy with a demon (17:14-21), Jesus' second prediction of his death and resurrection (17:22-23), and the coin in the fish's mouth (17:24-27). Throughout the chapter, Jesus and his disciples are in Galilee (where they have been, in fact, since chapter 13, when Jesus told his parables of the kingdom). Matthew begins the account of the coin in the fish's mouth by recording that they were now at Capernaum and that the collectors of the *dídrachma* (the annual two-drachma temple tax, equal to about two days' pay, required of each Jew) came to Peter with a question. "Doesn't your teacher pay the *dídrachma?*" they ask. Peter answers with a simple yes, but his meaning, presumably, is something like a "sure" or an "of course he does"—a quick reply, in other words, based more on Peter's own desire to make his master look respectable in the eyes of the authorities than on his actual knowledge of

Jesus' intentions. When Peter comes into the house, however, Jesus (who seems not to have been present at the interrogation) begins to speak about the temple tax before Peter says even a word. "What do you think, Simon?" he asks. "From whom do the kings of the earth take tax or tribute? *From their sons [huión] or from others [allotríon]?*"

The italicized words are difficult to translate. What I have given is a literal, but not strictly accurate, rendering. "Sons" is a Hebraism meaning not the literal children of the kings but the citizens of their dominions—much as the "sons of Israel" or "children of Israel" most often means simply "the people of Israel" or "the Israelites." What the text actually says, therefore, would be better represented by *"from their own citizens or from foreigners?"*—which is, with certain variations, the way most recent translators have Englished it. The difficulty with such a rendering, however, is that it makes precious little sense to a modern American reader. Ever since the invention of the income tax (not to mention the sales tax, the excise tax, and the Triborough Bridge and Tunnel Authority), those who have paid toll and tribute to the governing authorities of America have been not foreigners but the American citizenry themselves. Consequently, if "sons" is translated "citizens" and "others" is translated "foreigners," then when Peter says that kings take tribute from foreigners—and Jesus responds with the punch line of the whole parable, namely, "then the citizens are free"—all you will get from an American audience (or almost any other) is a cynical "Fat chance!" I propose, therefore, to put up with whatever strain may be involved in using the gnat-sized inaccuracy "sons" or "children" rather than swallow the correct but point-destroying camel of "citizens." After all, ninety-nine Americans out of a hundred are probably convinced that the Prince of Wales has no income-tax liability. Whether they are right or wrong as to the fact of that matter, only "sons" or "children" has any chance of communicating to them the note of freedom from religious liability that is, to me at least, the point of the whole parable.

Let me interrupt myself with a slight digression on the subject of literal versus periphrastic translation. Admittedly, one cannot always translate word for word from one language to another (try putting "knucklehead" into French literally). Nevertheless, there is something to be said, especially when dealing with complex and skillful authors, for trying as often as possible to give literal translations to at least their more important words.

In the case of the text we are dealing with, the choice of the Greek word *huión* ("sons") by Jesus (or Matthew, or the Spirit, or all three) involves a deliberate and complex play on the uses of the word "son" *(huiós)* in the preceding episodes. Let me list them. In Peter's confession (e.g., Matt. 16:13) Jesus asks his disciples, "Who do men say that the Son of man is?"—and when Peter replies (16:16), he says, "You are the Christ, the Son of the living God." In the first prediction of his death (e.g., Luke 9:22), Jesus refers to himself as the "Son of man." In the transfiguration (e.g., Matt. 17:5), God speaks out of the cloud and says, "This is my beloved Son." In the question about the coming of Elijah (17:12), Jesus again refers to the "Son of man"—and he does it once more (e.g., 17:22) in the second prediction of his death. In the light of all those passages, therefore, when Jesus refers to kings' tax-exempt citizens as "sons"—and then proceeds to tell Peter that "the sons are therefore free"—he is incorporating into his remark all the freight of the previous usages of the word "son." He means, of course, that the citizens of the messianic kingdom are free. But unless a translator indulges in extensive periphrasis to make that point clear, the use of any word other than "sons"—e.g., "citizens" (TEV), "family" (JBP), "own people" (NEB), or even "children" (KJV)—simply deprives the reader of the association with the sonship of Jesus himself on which the assertion of freedom is actually based. (For the record, the VgCL, the RSV, and the JB—which actually points out the play on words in a footnote—all opt for the literal rendering "sons.")

I raise this issue for several reasons. The first is based on what I have just said about not unnecessarily depriving the reader of associations present in the original text. Good authors expect their readers to build a mental concordance of every major word in their writings so that when a new twist is given to a word already used, the readers will be able to enter into and be enriched by the pun intended. But when translators make a habit of always rendering a word as what it *means* at a given point rather than as what it *is,* they derail authors from their purposes. In my view, therefore, the job of saying in detail what a text means should be left to expositors, exegetes, and preachers. Translators should content themselves with being as literal as they can be, short of setting down nonsense.

The second reason follows from that. The abundance of modern versions of the Scriptures has not been an unmixed blessing—as anyone who knows the Greek text will attest. It is a cautionary experience, for a teacher working from the Greek, to hand a Bible class half a dozen different English versions of, say, Matt. 17:24-27 and invite them to debate the meaning of the passage. More often than not, their natural inclination to take the English words in front of them as what the original really says tricks them into all kinds of fanciful, even false, starts as to what the passage might actually mean. And that happens most frequently, mind you, precisely when the versions used are ones whose guiding purpose was to translate what the Greek meant rather than what it said.

For ordinary study purposes, therefore, I direct students who do not know Greek to the more committedly literal versions (KJV and RSV), and to the TEV as a backup in case they want to check a little further as to meaning. But for major investigations of meaning, I urge them to use a concordance (such as *Young's* to the KJV) that has an index-lexicon to the original Hebrew and Greek. The advantage of this feature is tremendous: it enables the student to look up *every* use of a given Hebrew or Greek word, no matter how it was translated. Admittedly, in addition to those positive suggestions, I do have some unkind words to say about versions that strike me as unduly periphrastic, or as having been devised to advance the cause of particular religious movements or theological orthodoxies. Rather than name names here, however, I shall content myself with one all-encompassing observation: the work of dealing with the text itself is demanding enough; it is not made any easier when it has to be done through a programmatic overlay, or while wearing doctrinal mittens.

But back to the text at hand before this digression slips into mere pique. Jesus now (Matt. 17:27) shifts gears. Having told Peter that "the sons are therefore free"—that is, having established by the spoken part of his parable that neither he himself nor his brethren in the new order of his sonship are under any obligation to the old order represented by the authorities and their temple tax—he proceeds to the *acted* part of the parable. "In order that we don't scandalize them, though," he says, "go to the sea, cast in a hook, and take the first fish that comes up. When you open its mouth you will find a *statér* [a coin worth four drachmas]; take that and give it to them for me and you."

Let me get one useless question out of the way immediately. To those who ask, "Do you think this really happened?" I will answer yes and take whatever critical lumps I have to just to get off the subject. I can't prove I'm right, of course; but then neither can anyone else prove I'm wrong. Furthermore, there is no a priori system of biblical interpretation (except for the obviously wrong-headed one that says everything in the Bible must, ipso facto, be literally true) that can decide the issue one way or the other. The episode just sits there in the text, waiting to be commented on, not argued with. If it so happens that you find it impossible to swallow (as the fish, perhaps, found the *statér*), I respect that. Let's just agree to disagree about the moot point and get on with the more enjoyable business of playing, scripturally, with what's on the page.

My interpretation of the whole passage can be put briefly: Jesus, having arrived at the recognition that his own death will lie at the heart of his messiahship, finally feels free enough of the old political, religious, and ethical messianic expectations to make a joke about them. Not that he hadn't always sat loose to them to some degree (from the start, he broke the sabbath and consorted with morally unacceptable types); rather, he now finds himself totally beyond all the plausible, right-handed programs of salvation and therefore "free among the dead"—as well as among the last, the least, the lost, and the little, all of whom will loom large in the parables of grace he is about to unfold. The coin in the fish's mouth, therefore, is Jesus' first drawing in of the breath of utterly fresh air that he himself will ultimately be for the whole world.

Those, of course, are my words; Jesus probably never thought or felt about the matter in such terms. But the episode *is* a lark: he seems to be, for whatever reason, more at ease, more relaxed than before. He uses a kind of rabbinical whimsy to set Peter up; when Peter gives the obvious, right response, Jesus delivers a blithely sweeping declaration of independence; and to cap the climax, he concocts a hilarious mixture of consideration for others ("let's not scandalize them"), frivolous wonder-working ("take the first fish"), and financial precision ("you'll find a *statér*"—four drachmas, right on the nose). At the very least, therefore, he intimates what Paul would eventually express in so many words, namely, "the glorious liberty of the children of God" (Rom. 8:21).

On then with the scriptural playing around. I shall focus on only two elements in the story: the tax in question was the *temple* tax; and Jesus declares his (and our) freedom from it on the basis of *sonship*. Let me weave you a tissue of biblical quotations.

There are two words for temple in the New Testament: *hierón* (sacred place), referring either to the temple itself or to the temple precincts, and *naós* (from the verb *naíein,* to dwell), referring sometimes to the temple and sometimes to its inner sanctuary. Neither word actually occurs in the passage at hand; but since the word *dídrachma* had come to stand not only for a coin but for the temple tax that was paid with it, that word is quite sufficient to bring with it the freight of *religion* that Jesus, in my view, ultimately makes light of.

Consider the general picture. In a good many of the Gospel passages about the temple, Jesus is portrayed as putting a certain distance between himself and what the temple stood for in the religion of his day. He declines Satan's invitation (e.g., Matt. 4:5-6) to jump off a pinnacle of the temple *(hierón)* and be miraculously caught by angels. When his disciples pluck grain on the sabbath (Matt. 12:1-8), he justifies them by saying that the priests in the temple *(hierón)* profane the sabbath guiltlessly when they eat the bread of the presence and that, in any case, someone greater than the temple (namely, himself) is here. After his triumphal entry into Jerusalem, he goes into the temple *(hierón:* Matt. 21, Mark 11, Luke 19, John 2) and casts out the money-changers. (John, interestingly, puts this event early in Jesus' ministry rather than in Holy Week, thus giving it a "tone-setting" function similar to the one I am attributing to the coin in the fish's mouth in Matthew.) During the cleansing of the temple in John, Jesus says (at 2:19) "destroy this temple *[naós]* and I will raise it up in three days." (John says that Jesus meant the temple of his body—as no doubt he did; but nearly everyone took him to mean [see Matt. 26:61 and 27:40; Mark 14:58 and 15:29] the temple itself.) Finally, at his death (Matt. 27:51; Mark 15:38; Luke 23:45) the veil of the temple *(naós)* was torn in two—signifying, presumably, the end of the old religion of the temple by virtue of its fulfilment in the new mystery of Jesus' death.

One last reference to the temple *(hierón)* provides a bridge to the word "sons" or "children" as it appears in the episode of the coin in the fish's mouth. As a result of the healings Jesus did immediately after the cleansing of the temple, the high priests and the scribes became angry. They were upset, Matthew says (21:15), when they saw "the wonderful things he was doing, and the children *[paídas]* crying out in the temple, 'Hosanna to the Son *[huiô̂]* of David.'" So they said to him, "Do you hear what they are saying?" And Jesus said to them, "Yes. Haven't you ever read that 'Out of the mouths of babies *[népíōn]* and nursing children *[thēlazóntōn]* you have brought perfect praise?'"

Let me simply set down a list of the words in the New Testament that can be translated "son" or "child." There is *huiós* (son, descendant, offspring); *téknon* (child, descendant); *pais* (child, boy, servant); *paidíon* (little boy, lad); and there is *népios* (baby) and *thēlázōn* (suckling child), as cited above. Perhaps you see now why I am so strongly against "citizens" as a translation for "sons" *(huioi)*. And perhaps you also see why, despite what I said earlier, I now find myself hard put to decide between "sons" and "children" in translating Jesus' punch line in the parable of the coin in the fish's mouth. The RSV rendering ("Then the sons are free") does indeed catch the associations of the freedom with Jesus' own Sonship and thus with the mystery of death and resurrection that reigns in his (and our) filial relationship with his Father. But the KJV ("Then are the children free") seems to me not only less limiting as to gender but in particular more evocative of the rest of the "child" imagery in the New Testament.

Consider a few of the more salient examples. On a number of occasions, Jesus holds up a child *(paidíon)* as an example of the "littleness," etc., in which the mystery of his death and resurrection preeminently works. Again, he himself is referred to in the Book of Acts (3:13, 26; 4:27, 30) as God's holy *pais* (translated by the KJV as "son" or "child" and by the RSV and TEV as "servant"). Not only that, but this appellation occurs, remarkably enough, in connection with references to his crucifixion, thus making it evocative, once again, of lastness, leastness, lostness, littleness, and death. Finally, the remaining major word for "child" *(téknon)* brings into the picture the scriptural references to our share in the sonship (and thus in the passion) that is the root of the freedom of which Jesus is speaking. See, for example, John 1:12: "to them gave he the power to become the children *[tékna]* of God"; and Rom. 8:16-17: "the Spirit himself bears witness with our spirit that we are children *[tékna]* of God, and if children *[tékna],* then heirs as well—heirs of God and fellow heirs with Christ, provided we suffer with him in order that we might also be glorified with him."

But enough of this hammering home of specific scriptural words. The general thrust of my treatment of the coin in the fish's mouth—and especially of Jesus' words, "then the children are free"—is to interpret the whole passage as a proclamation of the end of religion. To me, the episode says that whatever it was that religion was trying to do (the religion of the temple in particular and, by extension, all religions everywhere) will not be accomplished by religious acts at all but in the mystery of Jesus' death and resurrection. As I said, that perception seems to have been so liberating to Jesus that he allowed himself the frivolity of this very odd miracle indeed. But beyond that, it is also (or at least it should be) radically liberating to everyone.

The entire human race is profoundly and desperately religious. From the dim beginnings of our history right up to the present day, there is not a man, woman, or child of us who has ever been immune to the temptation to think that the relationship between God and humanity can be repaired from our side, by our efforts. Whether those efforts involve creedal correctness, cultic performances, or ethical achievements—or whether they amount to little more than crassly superstitious behavior—we are all, at some deep level, committed to them. If we are not convinced that God can be conned into being favorable to us by dint of our doctrinal orthodoxy, or chicken sacrifices, or the gritting of our moral teeth, we still have a hard time shaking the belief that stepping over sidewalk cracks, or hanging up the bath towel so the label won't show, will somehow render the Ruler of the Universe kindhearted, softheaded, or both.

But as the Epistle to the Hebrews pointed out long ago, all such behavior is bunk. The blood of bulls and goats cannot take away sins, nor can any other religious act do what it sets out to do. Either it is ineffective for its purpose, or the supposedly effective intellectual, spiritual, or moral uprightness it counts on to do the job is simply unavailable. The point is, we haven't got a card in our hand that can take even a single trick against God. Religion, therefore—

despite the correctness of its insistence that something needs to be done about our relationship with God—remains unqualified bad news: it traps us in a game we will always and everywhere lose.

But the Gospel of our Lord and Savior Jesus Christ is precisely Good News. It is the announcement, in the death and resurrection of Jesus, that God has simply called off the game—that he has taken all the disasters religion was trying to remedy and, without any recourse to religion at all, set them to rights by himself. How sad, then, when the church acts as if it is in the religion business rather than in the Gospel-proclaiming business. What a disservice, not only to itself but to a world perpetually sinking in the quagmire of religiosity, when it harps on creed, cult, and conduct as the touchstones of salvation. What a perversion of the truth that sets us free (John 8:32) when it takes the news that while we were yet sinners, Christ died for us (Rom. 5:8), and turns it into a proclamation of God as just one more insufferable bookkeeper.

I realize this is a long fetch from the parable of the coin in the fish's mouth, but I make no apologies. In fact, I end with something even farther fetched. The Messiah whom Jesus' contemporaries expected—and likewise any and all of the messiahs the world has looked to ever since (even, alas, the church's all-too-often graceless, punishing version of Jesus' own messiahship)—are like nothing so much as religious versions of "Santa Claus is coming to town." The words of that dreadful Christmas song sum up perfectly the only kind of messianic behavior the human race, in its self-destructive folly, is prepared to accept: "He's making a list; he's checking it twice; he's going to find out who's naughty, or nice"—and so on into the dark night of all the tests this naughty world can never pass. For my money, what Jesus senses clearly and for the first time in the coin in the fish's mouth is that he is not, thank God, Santa Claus. He will come to the world's sins with no lists to check, no tests to grade, no debts to collect, no scores to settle. He will wipe away the handwriting that was against us and nail it to his cross (Col. 2:14). He will save, not some minuscule coterie of good little boys and girls with religious money in their piggy banks, but all the stone-broke, deadbeat, overextended children of this world whom he, as the Son of man—the holy Child of God, the Ultimate Big Kid, if you please—will set free in the liberation of his death.

And when he senses *that* . . . well, it is simply to laugh. He tacks a "Gone Fishing" sign over the sweatshop of religion, and for all the debts of all sinners who ever lived, he provides exact change for free. How nice it would be if the church could only remember to keep itself in on the joke.

CHAPTER FOUR

Losing as the Mechanism of Grace

The Lost Sheep

Admittedly, the coin in the fish's mouth may have struck you as a slightly "bent" episode to choose as an introduction to Jesus' parables of grace; but before proceeding to the first of his "straight" parables on the subject, the story of the lost sheep (Matt. 18:10-14; Luke 15:3-7; Aland no. 169), let me continue just a bit longer in the introductory mode. As you already know, I consider context to be crucial to the treatment of any parable. Accordingly, since I am following Matthew at this point, I want you to look at what occurs immediately preceding the parable in Matt. 18:1-9.

Jesus' disciples come to him (the setting is still Capernaum) and ask, "Who is the greatest in the kingdom of heaven?" The oddity of this question is more obvious in Mark (9:33-37) and Luke (9:46-48) than it is in Matthew. In those two Gospels, the episode (Aland no. 166) comes right after Jesus' second prediction of his passion (Aland no. 164), and it is reported as arising out of an argument among the disciples over which of them was the most important. (Matthew, for his own reasons, interposes the coin in the fish's mouth—Aland no. 165—between the two events.) In any case, the question they were debating is a prime example of the non-comprehension that bedeviled even the closest followers of Jesus. Observe. Jesus has just finished telling them in so many words that he, the Son of man, is going to die. They, however, unable to make any sense of such depressing talk from the mouth of one they have just recognized as the Messiah, simply change the subject to something happier. "Let's talk instead," they seem to say, "about how things will be when the messianic kingdom is finally accomplished. Who of us do you think will be number one?"

31

That, of course—given the generally low level of human performances on high subjects—produced more heat than light and
degenerated into mere one-upmanship. And Jesus, sensing the friction without even, as far as we can tell, being privy to the conten-
tion, brings up the subject by asking the loaded question, "What
were you discussing on the way?" (Mark 9:33). Mark observes that
the disciples (presumably out of embarrassment) simply didn't answer; but Jesus goes straight to the point anyway. If I may put all
three accounts into one, the episode is as follows. Jesus calls the
Twelve and says to them, "If anyone would be first, he must be last
[éschatos] of all and servant [diákonos] of all." Then he takes a child
(paidíon), puts him in the midst of them, and tells them that unless
they turn and become like children, they will never enter the kingdom at all—adding that whoever humbles himself like this child is
in fact the greatest in the kingdom of heaven. Finally, he says that
whoever receives one such child in his name receives not only him
but the one who sent him, and that "he who is the least [mikróteros,
littlest] among you is the one who is great."

I set this down as yet more evidence that Jesus, as he begins the
parables of grace, is preoccupied with the notion that the work of
the Messiah will be accomplished not by winning but by losing. Out
of the five items in my already often-repeated catalogue of "losing"
categories—the last (éschatos), the least (eláchistos), the lost (apolōlós),
the little (mikrós), and the dead (nekrós)—he has, in a mere handful
of verses, just ticked off no less than three. Not only that, but in
holding up as his example a little boy (or girl—the Greek word
paidíon is actually a neuter diminutive), he has included the note of
little-childhood I have already alluded to (see above, pp. 17-18 and
27-28) and which Jesus again and again emphasizes (for instance,
Matt. 19:13-15 and parallels, and the opening line of the upcoming
parable of the Lost Sheep, Matt. 18:10.)

Moreover, in Mark 9:38-41 and Luke 9:49-50 (Aland
no. 167), he continues in the same vein. The disciples, even after
Jesus has just finished exalting losers over winners, still haven't an
inkling of what he's getting at. One of them, John, immediately
changes the subject, providing yet another example of incomprehension. "Master," he says, "we saw a man casting out
demons in your name, and we forbade him because he was not
following us." True enough, John probably thought he was picking

up on Jesus' words about being "sent"; but most likely, he was in fact dismayed at this man's lack of proper accreditation—at his status as an inferior to the duly authorized Twelve. John's view, in other words, was that anyone who did Jesus' work should be a winner who could pass the merit-badge test for Official Exorcist; he was totally unprepared to give anything more than the cold shoulder to an unlicensed loser.

Jesus, however, simply tells John (Luke 9:50) not to run around forbidding such people. "He who is not against you is for you," he says—implying, as I read it, that none of the acceptability tests John has in mind has any bearing on Jesus' way of going about the business of the kingdom. "So what if the man is an outsider and therefore a loser," Jesus seems to ask; "haven't I just gotten through saying that I myself, the Messiah, am going to be the biggest outsider and loser of all? Don't you think it's about time you stopped being scandalized by what you consider my lack of messianic respectability and just listen to me for a change?"

That thought, logically enough, brings us to the very next bit of context (Matt. 18:6-9; Mark 9:42-50; Aland no. 168). Jesus says that "if anyone scandalizes [skandalísē] one of these little ones [mikrōn] who believes in me, it would be better for him to have a great millstone tied around his neck and be sunk to the bottom of the sea." To me, the most natural referent of the mikrōn in this remark is the unofficial exorcist the disciples have just referred to: he is precisely one of the "little losers" about whom Jesus has been, and still is, talking. The word skandalísē, however, needs more attention.

The verb skandalízein means, variously, to cause someone to stumble, sin, give up his faith; to give offense or scandal; or to throw difficulties in someone's way. The KJV, for example, renders it "offend"; the RSV, "cause to sin"; the TEV, "cause to turn away." In any case, it seems to me that the precise offense or cause of turning away that Jesus has in mind is the despising of the littleness, lostness, lastness, etc., that he has been working up into a veritable catalogue of redeeming unsuccesses. "Don't go around throwing their littleness or lack of respectability at them," he says in effect, "because those things are my chosen métier. If you spook them away from such things, you spook them away from me. I just can't use you if you insist on behaving like that. You'd be better off dead—which, incidentally, happens to be the only condition I'm ultimately going to bother with anyway."

Furthermore, he follows that up with what I see as variations on the same theme. "Woe to the world," he says (Matt. 18:7), "because of these turnings away [skándala]. Such skándala will always come [because, as I read it, Jesus' insistence on unsuccess will always be radically unacceptable to people in their right, success-loving minds] but woe to the man [and specifically, to the disciple] by whom the skándalon comes." In other words, any disciple of Jesus who enlists on the side of the world's winners will simply have cut himself off from the losers who alone have the keys to the kingdom; worse yet, he himself will inevitably become just another doomed winner.

And Jesus drives that point home with some bizarre imagery. "If your hand or your foot causes you to turn away," he says (that is, if being a winner with success-oriented equipment causes you to forget that I work through losers only), "then cut it off: it's better for you to enter into life maimed or lame [in other words, to live as a loser in this age] than to end up having your whole unredeeming and unredeemed success thrown in the fire of the age to come."

But then, after one more illustration about plucking out an eye if it causes this same turning away, Jesus sums up his argument with a mini-parable on salt (Mark 9:49-50; Luke 14:34-35—with the parallel passage at Matt. 5:13). "You are the salt of the earth," he says (I am using the Matthean reading), "but if the salt has become insipid [mōranthé—literally, become foolish], what in the world is there that can restore saltness to it? It is good for nothing except to be thrown out and trampled on by people [anthrópōn, men]."

Consider the imagery. Salt seasons and salt preserves, but in any significant quantity, it is not of itself edible, nourishing, or pleasant. On the basis of Jesus' comparison, therefore, we are presumably meant to understand that neither his paradoxical messiahship nor his disciples' witness to it (assuming they don't betray it with sugary substitutes) will be all that appetizing to the world. People simply do not come in droves to anyone who insists that the only way to win is to lose. Nevertheless, Jesus' teaching is exactly that salty: "The disciple is not above his teacher," he told his followers (e.g., Matt. 10:24-25); "it is enough for the disciple to be like his teacher." And he went on to spell out the meaning of that assertion in his very first prediction of his death (e.g., Matt. 16:24-25): "If anyone wants to come with me, let him deny himself, take up his cross, and follow me. For if anyone wants to save his life, he will lose *[apolései]* it; and whoever loses his life for my sake will find it."

But if the salt of the earth becomes insipid—if a disciple of Jesus forgets that only losing wins, and a fortiori, if the apostolic church forgets it—where in the wide world of winners drowning in the syrup of their own success will either the disciple or the church be able to recapture the saltiness of victory out of loss? The answer is nowhere. And the sad fact is that the church, both now and at far too many times in its history, has found it easier to act as if it were selling the sugar of moral and spiritual achievement rather than the salt of Jesus' passion and death. It will preach salvation for the successfully well-behaved, redemption for the triumphantly correct in doctrine, and pie in the sky for all the winners who think they can walk into the final judgment and flash their passing report cards at Jesus. But every last bit of that is now and ever shall be pure baloney because: (a) nobody will ever have that kind of sugar to sweeten the last deal with, and (b) Jesus is going to present us all to the Father in the power of *his* resurrection and not at all in the power of our own totally inadequate records, either good or bad.

But does the church preach that salty message? Not as I hear it, it doesn't. It preaches the nutra-sweet religion of test-passing, which is the only thing the world is ready to buy and which isn't even real sugar let alone salt. In spite of all our fakery, though, Jesus' program remains firm. He saves losers and only losers. He raises the dead and only the dead. And he rejoices more over the last, the least, and the little than over all the winners in the world. That alone is what this losing race of ours needs to hear, even though it can't stand the thought of it. That alone is the salt that can take our perishing insipidity and give it life and flavor forever. That alone. . . .

But why hammer half-moons into the woodwork when Jesus drives the point home with one square blow? We have arrived at the parable of the Lost Sheep—and as you may suspect, I have very nearly finished my exposition before even starting it. Let me simply comment on the highlights of the parable as they now appear.

In Matthew (18:10-11), Jesus begins the parable with the already cited, "Watch that you don't despise one of these little ones *[mikrón],* for I tell you that their angels in heaven always behold the

face of my Father who is in heaven." (Whatever it may have been
that these last words were alluding to in the theology of Jesus' times,
they at least say clearly enough that it is precisely the little, and not
the big, who have an abiding relationship with God.) Furthermore,
Matthew has Jesus continue in the same vein in verse 11: "For the
Son of man came to save the lost *[apolōlós]*." This verse, which is
absent from the oldest and best manuscripts we have, is still worthy
of some kind of inclusion. For the record, the KJV and VgCL put it
in the text, the TEV sets it in square brackets, and the RSV, NEB,
and JB print it as a footnote. In any case, the verse simply puts one
more accent on the "lostness" already stressed throughout the passages at hand.

When Luke introduces the parable of the Lost Sheep (in
15:1-3), he puts the same emphasis on losers in a different but
equally definite way. He records that tax collectors *(telṓnai)* and
sinners *(hamartōloí)* were coming to Jesus to hear him, and that the
Pharisees and scribes (winners all) grumbled extensively about such
consorting with losers. "This man welcomes outcasts *[hamartōloí]*,"
they murmur, "and even eats with them" (verses 1 and 2, TEV). And
Luke completes his introduction (in verse 3) by saying, "So Jesus
told them this parable." In other words, the parable is presented as
yet another instance of Jesus' rubbing the salt of lostness on the
sensibilities of those who are preoccupied with the sweetness of
their own success.

As far as the parable itself is concerned, Matthew and Luke give
only slightly differing versions. Jesus begins by proposing to his
audience (to the disciples, presumably, in Matthew; to the Pharisees
and scribes in Luke) a hypothetical case. Suppose, he suggests to
them, a man has a hundred sheep and one of them gets lost (Matthew says it "goes astray"—*planēthḗ*; Luke says "he loses"—*apo-
lésas*—it). Jesus then asks (expecting, of course, an affirmative answer), "Won't the man leave the ninety-nine on the mountain [Luke
says, 'in the desert'] and go and seek the stray [Luke has 'the lost']?"

Time for a pause. While it may or may not be true that shep-
herds in Jesus' day had that kind of devotion to individual members
of their flocks, this parable can hardly be interpreted as a helpful hint
for running a successful sheep-ranching business. The most likely
result of going off in pursuit of one lost sheep will only be ninety-
nine more lost sheep. Accordingly, I think it best to assume that

Jesus is parabolically thumping the tub for the saving paradox of lostness. He implies, it seems to me, that even if all one hundred sheep should get lost, it will not be a problem for this bizarrely Good Shepherd because he is first and foremost in the business of finding the lost, not of making a messianic buck off the unstrayed. Give him a world with a hundred out of every hundred souls lost—give him, in other words, the worldful of losers that is the only real world we have—and it will do just fine: lostness is exactly his cup of tea. (Incidentally, the "ninety-nine just persons who need no repentance" whom Jesus adduces later in the parable are strictly a rhetorical device: in fact, there are not and never have been any such people anywhere.)

No matter what we do with lostness, though, the rest of the parable is about one thing and one thing only: joy *(chará)*, which is the root and blossom of the shepherd's will to find. This note is clearer, perhaps, in Luke than in Matthew, but it is the whole point of both. Matthew has Jesus say simply that the man rejoices *(chaírei)* more over the one than over the ninety-nine who had not strayed; in Luke, Jesus paints a vivid picture of the joy, complete with the man putting the sheep on his shoulders, coming back to his house, calling together his friends and neighbors, and saying, "Rejoice *[syncháreté]* with me, for I have found my lost *[apolōlós]* sheep."

It is at the very end of the parable, however, that Jesus makes his point most strongly. Pushing his comparison all the way to heaven itself, he says (Matt. 18:14), "Thus it is not the will of my Father who is in heaven that one of these little ones *[mikrón]* should perish *[apólētai]*." These words need no more comment than I have already given them; but in Luke (15:7), Jesus gives his summation in a way that cries out for further exposition. "Thus," he says, "there will be more joy in heaven over one sinner who repents than over ninety-nine just persons who need no repentance." Time out now for a full-scale halt on the subject of repentance as it arises in Jesus' parables of joy at finding the lost.

To begin with, let me enter into the record at this point the parable of the Lost Coin. It appears only in Luke (at 15:8-10; Aland no. 220), and it is presented there as a variation on the immediately preceding parable of the Lost Sheep. Jesus begins in the same hypothetical way ("what woman, if she has ten drachmas . . ."), and he continues with the same suggestion that she will drop everything and hunt energetically for the lost property. When she finds it, Jesus says, she too calls friends and neighbors together and says, "Rejoice *[synchá;rēté]* with me, for I have found the drachma I lost *[apólesa]*." Finally, Jesus concludes the parable (at verse 10) with substantially the same observation as before: "Thus, I say to you, there is joy before the angels of God over one repentant *[metanooúnti]* sinner."

It is usual, when expounding the word *metanoéein* (repent), to go about the job etymologically. Since the word is a compound of *metá* (after) and *noéein* (think), its root meaning is to change one's mind or, better said, to change one's heart about one's sins. That approach, however, does not serve well here. Neither the lost coin nor the lost sheep was capable of any repentance at all. The entire cause of the recovery operation in both stories is the shepherd's, or the woman's, determination to find the lost. Neither the lost sheep nor the lost coin does a blessed thing except hang around in its lostness. On the strength of this parable, therefore, it is precisely our sins, and not our goodnesses, that most commend us to the grace of God.

Hence if in our interpretations we harp on the necessity of a change of heart—if we badger ourselves with the dismal notion that sinners must first forsake their sins before God will forgive them, that the lost must somehow find itself before the finder will get up off his backside and look for it—we carry ourselves straight away from the obvious sense of both stories. And since that violates not only the parables but also Rom. 5:8 ("while we were still sinners, Christ died for us"), I propose to take a different tack altogether and to look not at etymologies but simply at the stories as Jesus tells them.

Consider the following propositions, all of which I think are true. A lost sheep is, for all practical purposes, a dead sheep; a lost coin is likewise a dead asset. In addition (if I may look forward a bit to the parables of the Unforgiving Servant and of the Prodigal Son), a debtor about to be foreclosed on is a dead duck and a son who has blown his inheritance is a deadbeat. These parables of lostness, therefore, are far from being exhortations to repentance. They are emphatically not stories designed to convince us that if we will wind ourselves up to some acceptable level of moral and/or spiritual improvement, God will *then* forgive us; rather they are parables about God's determination to move *before* we do—in short, to make lostness and death the only tickets we need to the Supper of the Lamb. In all of them, it is precisely the lost (and thus the dead) who come to the party; in none of them is any of the unlost (and thus the living) in on the festivities. More than that, in none of these parables is *anything* (except the will of God) portrayed as necessary to the new life in joy. Neither the lostness, nor the deadness, nor the repentance is in itself redemptive; God alone gives life, and he gives it freely and fully on no conditions whatsoever. These stories, therefore, are parables of grace and grace only. There is in them not one single note of earning or merit, not one breath about rewarding the rewardable, correcting the correctible, or improving the improvable. There is only the gracious, saving determination of the shepherd, the woman, the king, and the father—all surrogates for God—*to raise the dead*.

That, I think, puts repentance—and confession, and contrition, and absolution, and all their ancillary subjects—in a different light. Confession, for example, turns out to be something other than we thought. It is not the admission of a mistake which, thank God and our better nature, we have finally recognized and corrected. Rather it is the admission that we are *dead* in our sins—that we have no power of ourselves either to save ourselves or to convince anyone else that we are worth saving. It is the recognition that our whole life is finally and forever *out of our hands* and that if we ever live again, our life will be entirely the gift of some gracious other.

And to take the other side of the coin, absolution too becomes another matter. It is neither a response to a suitably worthy confession, nor the acceptance of a reasonable apology. *Absolvere* in Latin means not only to loosen, to free, to acquit; it also means to dispose of, to complete, to finish. When God pardons, therefore, he does not say he understands our weakness or makes allowances for our errors; rather he disposes of, he finishes with, the whole of our dead life and raises us up with a new one. He does not so much deal with our derelictions as he does drop them down the black hole of Jesus' death. He forgets our sins in the darkness of the tomb. He remembers our iniquities no more in the oblivion of Jesus' expiration. He finds us, in short, in the desert of death, not in the garden of improvement; and in the power of Jesus' resurrection, he puts us on his shoulders rejoicing and brings us home.

CHAPTER FIVE

Death, Resurrection, and Forgiveness

The Unforgiving Servant

I felt free to raise the topic of forgiveness at the end of the last chapter precisely because the very next parable (the Unforgiving Servant, Matt. 18:21-35; Aland nos. 172-173) is one of Jesus' major treatments of the subject. But my tying of forgiveness to the raising of the dead—my insistence that it is a gift given to the totally incompetent, not a reward bestowed on the suitably disposed—may need more explanation.

When Jesus speaks about forgiveness (and above all, when he acts to bring it about), he bases his most telling words and deeds squarely on death and resurrection. Consider only two examples, the parable of the Prodigal Son and the crucifixion. In the first, Jesus is at pains to point out that the gift of forgiveness proceeds solely out of God's love and is therefore antecedent to any qualifying action on the part of the receiver (before the prodigal gets even a word of confession out of his mouth, the father runs, throws his arms around his son, and kisses him—Luke 15:20). And in the crucifixion, God in Christ acts strictly "for the joy that was set before him" (Heb. 12:2), enduring the cross and despising the shame for an entire race that was stone-cold dead in its sins (cf., e.g., Rom. 5:8, 12, 21). He waits, in other words, for nothing: not for repentance and certainly not for reform. He asks for no response, no life glued halfway back together, before he extends his pardon; he needs only the death that sin has caused, for the simple reason that the power of Jesus' resurrection does everything else that needs doing.

I set this down because while the note of unmerited grace raising the dead is clear enough in the parable of the Unforgiving Servant, it is not nearly so obvious in the sayings of Jesus (Matt.

18:15-20; Luke 17:3-4; Aland nos. 170-171) that immediately precede the parable. In the Lukan version, in fact, forgiveness seems quite simply to be made conditional on repentance: "Be on your guard!" Jesus says. "If your brother sins, rebuke him, and if he repents, forgive him. And if he sins seven times a day against you, and turns to you seven times and says, 'I repent,' you must forgive him."

In fairness, of course, even Luke's version (especially in view of the opening words, "Be on your guard!") should probably be interpreted chiefly as an insistence that Jesus' disciples must set no cutoff point for forgiveness—that they may never allow sin, however protracted or repeated, to have any effect on their determination to pardon. In short, it is unforgivingness, not subsequent sin, that is portrayed here as real abuse of the Gospel of forgiveness. But since Luke includes neither the parable of the Unforgiving Servant nor the Matthean buildup to it, the very brevity of the passage causes repentance-as-a-condition to leap to the eye of the reader.

When we turn to Matthew, however, we initially find ourselves confronted with a passage even more difficult than the one in Luke. For immediately after the parable of the Lost Sheep (with its conclusion, "thus it is not the will of your Father in heaven that one of these little ones should perish"), Matthew (18:15-17) gives us a discourse in which Jesus apparently reneges on everything he's established since chapter 16. "If your brother sins against you," he says, "go and rebuke him just between the two of you. If he listens to you, you have gained your brother. But if he refuses to listen to you, take with you one or two others, so that 'every accusation may be upheld by the testimony of two or three witnesses.' But if he refuses to listen to them, tell it to the church; and if he refuses to listen to the church, let him be to you as a Gentile and a tax collector."

"So much," Jesus seems to be saying, "for the losers of this world. Sure, I seek them as a shepherd seeks his lost sheep. But I'm not about to overdo it. What I really have in mind is that you should give your personal lost sheep—your sinning brother—exactly and only three shots at getting found. If he doesn't make it under that wire, you just tell him, 'Tough luck, Charlie.'"

Indeed, it is precisely on the strength of this and other apparently hard-nosed passages that the church worked up its two-thousand-year love affair with excommunication—its gleeful enthusiasm for running persistent strays off the Good Shepherd's ranch. But since that whole approach makes hash not only of the preceding parable of the Lost Sheep but also of the upcoming one on the Unforgiving Servant—and since I have already expressed my reluctance to conclude that the Gospel writers just dumped pericopes every which where without regard to context—I am not about to take such an interpretation lying down. I invite your attention, therefore, to what strikes me as the crucial bit of context here, namely, Jesus' final words in verse 17: "Let him be to you as a Gentile and a tax collector."

Some people have an odd idea of what constitutes fair exegesis. To them, the only thing you can do with "Gentile and tax collector" is read the words in the sense they presumably had for the average Jew of Jesus' day. Accordingly, such exegetes think that because Jesus' compatriots would have thought "outcast" when they heard the phrase, Jesus himself had to have been thinking about excommunication when he uttered it. But such an approach is a short stack of half-baked waffles.

The first waffle is precisely the failure of this sort of exegesis to pay attention to context: Jesus has just finished talking about actively seeking outcasts, not about giving them the boot. Therefore, even if he was actually thinking "outcast" when he said "Gentile and tax collector," it is quite unwarranted to conclude that he was telling his disciples to shun such types. The other waffle is its failure to pay attention to who is talking: Jesus was *not* an average Jew—and he was, by now, not an average Messiah either. His previous performances (sabbath-breaking, sniping at the establishment, hanging out with undesirables) were unconventional in the extreme. Thus there was at least a strong possibility that "Gentile and tax collector," from his mouth, might have had a non-excommunicatory meaning. Above all, though—and this, to me, clinches the case against these two waffles—who, in fact, were the undesirables Jesus hung around with? Were they not precisely "sinners of the Gentiles" (cf. Gal. 2:15) and tax collectors?

In other words, who says that exegesis is only fair if it's based on some critic's guess about what Jesus might possibly have *thought*? How come what he actually *did* can't govern the interpretation? Even if the critics could prove that Jesus couldn't possibly have thought what I take him to mean, so what? The fact remains that he did more than just think; if I want to understand the significance of his remarks from his life as a whole, what's to stop me? On at least one occasion (when he asked to have the crucifixion called off in the Garden of Gethsemane), his actions spoke louder than his words; who's to say that couldn't have been true on other occasions as well?

Consequently, I am going to let Jesus' actual behavior govern my reading of these verses: since he actively sought out the Gentiles and tax collectors he adduces here as apparent candidates for rejection, *I propose to take his words as ironic.* Consider, if you will, the dynamics of the situation. Jesus has been harping for some time on lostness, lastness, death, and the rest; but he is also acutely aware that his disciples hardly understand him at all. He develops a strategy, therefore: he will sucker them into revealing their incomprehension by giving them, as his own seemingly serious teaching, a string of propositions that will sound like nothing so much as a retraction of what he's been saying. He follows up his story of a really indefatigable seeker of the lost—of a shepherd who risks everything to find a single stray—with a series of "rules for limited forgiveness" that could have been written by the Committee for the Prevention of Wear and Tear on the Righteous. In other words, the whole thing is a setup: what Jesus is about to say is so obviously at odds with what he has just been saying that even apostolic dummies will sense the incongruity. But when they try to respond to his obviously erroneous rules with emendations based on their inadequate grasp of what true forgiveness involves, they will be forced to recognize that they failed utterly to understand him. The gambit, as clever as it is simple, goes like this (White is Jesus; Black, the disciples):

White:	". . . so the shepherd seeks the lost sheep unconditionally."
Black:	"You don't really mean that as practical advice, do you?"
White:	"Okay, so I'll make it practical. Forget the first story. The shepherd in the new parable gives the stupid sheep three chances to get found; then he gives up on it."
Black:	"Hey, maybe that's a little tougher than you meant to be. How about, he gives it seven chances?"

White: "Aha! Gotcha! How above seventy times seven? And how about checkmate? You thought I didn't really mean unconditionally, huh?"

That bit of whimsy, of course, catapults us straight from "Gentile and tax collector" (Matt. 18:17) to the question by Peter (18:21) that leads Jesus straight into the parable of the Unforgiving Servant. The intervening verses, however, while they are every bit as susceptible of hard-nosed interpretation as the passage we have just dealt with, deserve at least an attempt to give them a lenient reading.

Take verse 18 first: "Amen, I say to you whatever you bind on earth will be bound in heaven, and whatever you loose on earth will be loosed in heaven." I am sure no one needs reminding that this passage (along with John 20:23) has traditionally been the basis for the idea that the church can not only grant but also withhold absolution. For the record, though, I feel bound to point out that that particular doctrinal development does not seem to be consistent with the church's proclamation in the Nicene Creed that it acknowledges "one baptism for the forgiveness of sins." I take that phrase to mean that in baptism we are clothed, once and for all, with a forgiveness woven for us by Jesus' death and resurrection. The grace of baptism, therefore, is quite fittingly referred to as *habitual* grace (from "habit" as in "a nun's habit") because we wear it, all our lives long, as an irremovable vestment of forgiveness.

Accordingly, the church's creedal teaching seems to be that no matter what sins we commit subsequent to baptism, every last one of them is committed *inside* an effective suit of pardon that we can neither lose nor undo. To be sure, sinners can refuse to believe they are wearing the suit—and they can even, by refusing to forgive others, set themselves at cross-purposes with the suit; but I do not think we ought to talk as if the church, on its own motion, has any power to remove the suit by withholding absolution. (As a matter of fact, the church's own ancient insistence that baptism should never be repeated, even after grave sin, seems to argue for the same conclusion.)

Just what does this passage about binding and loosing mean then? Well, if you accept my view that Jesus was being ironic when he suggested that a sinning brother should be given only three whacks at forgiveness, these words show him dropping the irony and saying, seriously and plainly, what will happen if anyone follows such an unforgiving, unshepherdlike course.

Jesus flags this change of tone by the very first word in verse 18: the "Amen" is his standard trick of speech for calling attention to an utterly serious pronouncement. "Now listen up real good," he says in effect, "because I've been stringing you along. All that plausible advice about excommunicating the recalcitrant is hazardous to your health. Because if you go around binding your brother's sins on him, if you insist that beyond three months or three thousand miles of sinning his warranty of forgiveness will run out—if, in short, you treat him like an outcast instead of joining him in his lostness as I have joined Gentiles and tax collectors in theirs—then the deadly rule of unforgiveness will be all you have, here or hereafter. But if you loose his sins, if you move toward him in unconditional, un-limited forgiveness, then the life-giving rule of grace will prevail, both now on earth and forever in heaven."

The rest of the passage (Matt. 18:19-20), while a bit more obscure, is at least susceptible of the same reading. "Again I say to you," Jesus continues (the "again," I take it, serves as a repetition of the "amen"); "if two of you agree on earth about anything they ask, it will be done for them by my Father in heaven. For where two or three are gathered together in my name, there I am in the midst of them." Since these words stand just before the parable of the Un-forgiving Servant—and since they are the capstone of the whole passage (Matt. 18:15-20) immediately following the story of the Lost Sheep—I think it only fair to assume that their primary refer-ence is to the way forgiveness seeks out the lost. (That they can also have other meanings, I do not doubt; I am simply concerned here to put first things first.) Accordingly, I take them to mean that if two of Jesus' disciples—if, that is, his followers in their plural capacity as his witnessing church—agree to forgive rather than to excommuni-cate, then the Father will ratify and confirm their decision with all the power of his grace. And he will do that precisely because wher-ever two or three are gathered together in Jesus' name (that is, wherever the witnessing church is), there is Jesus himself, the friend of publicans and sinners, the Good Shepherd who lays down his life for the sheep, the beloved Son in whom the Father sees his whole creation forgiven and made new.

Before proceeding, though, let me add a note about the witnessing church to which Jesus, in my interpretation, has just referred. As I see it, the church's witness is at least threefold: kerygmatic, baptismal, and eucharistic. It is kerygmatic because the church is commissioned to proclaim the original apostolic preaching *(kērygma)*, namely, the announcement to the world of Jesus' resurrection from the dead. It is baptismal because the church is constituted as a living sign of that resurrection by the baptism in which its members die and rise in Jesus. And it is eucharistic because as often as two, or three, or any number of his followers "do this in remembrance of him," he is present among them in all the gracious power of his death and resurrection. At least tangentially, therefore, the passage at hand ends (Matt. 18:20) with a eucharistic note, and so with one more hint of the interrelationship in the Gospels between death-resurrection and grace-reconciliation.

That brings us, both logically and in terms of the text itself, to the parable of the Unforgiving Servant (Matt. 18:21-35). Since I have already commented on Jesus' emphasis (verses 21-22) on unlimited as opposed to limited forgiveness—on his tricking Peter into proposing a generous seven chances for forgiveness and then sending him sprawling with a bizarre insistence on seventy times seven—let me go straight to the story.

Jesus begins it by tying what he is about to say to the unconditional forgiveness he has just called for. *"Diá toúto,"* he says (on account of this, because of this, therefore), "the kingdom of heaven is like a king who wanted to settle accounts with his servants." Jesus, shrewd teacher that he is, begins by setting up law, not grace, as the first element of the parable. This king is a bookkeeper, pure and simple: for the honest, for the upright, and above all, for the solvent, he will have kind words; but for anyone in real trouble, he will have no care at all except to get his money back as best he can. Accordingly, when the stone-broke servant who owes him ten thousand talents is brought in (the amount of the debt is set at an astronomical ten million dollars or so to stress its radical unrepayability), the king orders him to be sold, lock, stock, barrel, wife, and children, and restitution to be made. There is no forgiveness in the story so far and there is no reason to expect it. It is all a matter of cut your losses and get out.

But then the servant falls on his knees before his master and says, "Have patience with me [*makrothýmēson, be big-hearted*] and I will repay you everything." And sure enough, the king's attitude suddenly changes. He goes straight from having had all the mercy of a loan shark to being a softy. "Taking pity," Jesus says (the Greek is *splanchnistheís, from splánchna, the bowels*, the seat of compassion), "the lord of that servant released him and forgave [*aphēken*] him the debt." Enter here, therefore, gut reaction rather than head reaction—or if you like, left-handed, right-brain activity as opposed to right-handed, left-brain activity—as the new basis of the king's behavior. But enter here also an even more important principle: the servant has to do nothing more than ask for grace to get grace. It is not that he earns it by extravagantly promising to repay everything at some future date. It is simply that the king cancels the debt *for reasons entirely internal to himself.*

Examine that last point more closely. The servant (closet bookkeeper that he is) no doubt thinks that his master is actually responding to his ridiculous offer of repayment. He has, in other words, not a shred of the notion of grace in his own mind. Like all desperate sinners, he knows only that he is in a tight spot and that he can't escape without outside help. But when he comes to imagine for himself what kind of "outsider" he needs to get him out of his bind, he can't think of anyone who isn't exactly like himself. Hence his con job about repayment: he assumes that the king is not only a bookkeeper interested solely in money, but also a stupid bookkeeper who can't spot a losing proposition when it slithers up to him. The servant knows he needs salvation, but the only savior he can imagine is someone who, except for dumb luck, would long ago have ended up as much in need of saving as himself.

The king, however, responds to nothing that the servant has in mind. He ignores the manifest nonsense about repayment. He makes no calculations at all about profit and loss. Instead, he simply drops dead to the whole business of bookkeeping and forgives the servant. Wipes the debt out. Forgets it ever existed. Does, in short, what the servant couldn't even conceive of doing. And do you know why the king could do that and the servant couldn't? Because the king was willing to end his old life of bookkeeping and the servant wasn't. Indeed, the servant was so busy trying to hold together his own bookkeeper's existence—so unable to imagine anything even vaguely like dropping dead to it—that he never even saw what the king had done. All he knew was that the heat, which formerly had been on, was now off. He hadn't the slightest notion of what it had cost the king to put out the fire.

You complain, perhaps, that I have once again dragged in death and resurrection by the hair of the head. I make no apology; both of them are integral to this parable. For one thing, the king does indeed die to the life he had when the story began: he goes out of the debt-collecting business altogether. For another, the servant's failure to perceive the king's death in the first half of the story is actually the only thing that can make sense of his otherwise incomprehensible mercilessness to his fellow servant in the second half. Consider, therefore, this bizarre unforgivingness that gives the parable its name.

The commonest objection to Jesus' parabolic picture of the servant's pitilessness is that it sets up a cardboard figure of wickedness. "How could anyone outside a comic book," we ask ourselves, "actually fail to see that if you've just been forgiven a multimillion-dollar debt—and freed from slavery to boot—you don't first-off go and try to beat a hundred bucks out of somebody who's still a slave?" The unforgiving servant, however, is anything but a cartoon villain; he is, in fact, exactly what everybody else in the world is, namely, an average citizen totally unwilling to face death in any way. Not only hasn't he paid attention to his lord's death to a lifetime of bookkeeping; he's also totally unwilling to accept the death the king has handed him in setting him free. Note that last point well: in spite of the fact that he was an important enough servant to run up a whopping debt (mere stableboys don't have opportunities like that), his first thought on being released was not how to die to his old life and market himself in a new one. Rather it was to go on with all his bookkeeping as before. Hence, with deathless logic, he puts the arm on his fellow servant. And hence he misses the whole new life he might have lived out of death.

And so do we, when we refuse death. Jesus has not only set Peter up in this passage; he has set us up as well. He has been saying with utter clarity that he, the Messiah, is going to solve the world's problems by dying. His answer to our sins will be the oblivion of a death on the cross. His response to our loss of control over our destinies will be to lose everything himself. What he tells us in this parable, therefore, is that unless we too are willing to see our own death as the one thing necessary to our salvation—unless we can, unlike the unforgiving servant, die to the gimcrack accounts by which we have justified our lives—we will never be able to enjoy the resurrection, even though Jesus hands it to us on a silver platter. If we cannot face the price he has paid to free us, we might as well never have been freed at all.

The remaining details of the parable make that clear. The unforgiving servant's fellow slaves see his unmerciful behavior and are greatly distressed. They understand what the king has done. They know that he has laid down vast royal prerogatives—that, as far as the indebted servant is concerned, he has rolled over and played dead. And they see clearly what an outrage, what a violation of grace it is when the servant is unwilling to lay down even the two-bit prerogatives he himself has. So they come and tell their lord all that has taken place; and the lord summons the servant and confronts him with his refusal to die. "You wicked servant!" he shouts at him in anger. "I forgave you all that debt just because you asked me to. Don't you think you should have had mercy [eleésai] on your fellow servant, as I had mercy [éléēsa] on you?"

In other words, the king sets before the servant the two scenes he has just been through and he rubs the salt of them into the wound of the servant's refusal to die. In each, there was a creditor with lawful rights; in each, a plea for patience from the debtor and a promise to repay. But then the king drives home the one, crucial difference. "I *died* for you, for Christ's sake!" he says; "but you were so busy making plans for your stupid life, you never even noticed." And therefore the king pronounces judgment on him. Because the servant has chosen a losing life instead of a gracious death, the king condemns him to just that life: he delivers him to the torturers, to be tormented until he pays the debt—which means, obviously, for his whole life, until death itself does for him what he refused to do on his own.

Jesus then ends the parable with a confirmation of that same judgment: "So also my heavenly Father will do to you, if you do not each forgive his brother from your heart." Interestingly, therefore, this parable of grace ends as a parable of judgment as well—and it makes clear, long before we get to the parables of judgment themselves, the only basis on which anyone will be finally condemned. None of our debts—none of our sins, none of our trespasses, none of our errors—will ever be an obstacle to the grace that raises the dead. At the most, they will be the measure of our death, and as soon as we die, they too will be dead, because our Lord the King has already died to them. But if we refuse to die—and in particular, if we insist on binding others' debts upon them in the name of our own right to life—we will, by not letting grace have its way *through* us, cut ourselves off from ever knowing the joy of grace *in* us.

In heaven, there are only forgiven sinners. There are no good guys, no upright, successful types who, by dint of their own integrity, have been accepted into the great country club in the sky. There are only failures, only those who have accepted their deaths in their sins and who have been raised up by the King who himself died that they might live.

But in hell, too, there are only forgiven sinners. Jesus on the cross does not sort out certain exceptionally recalcitrant parties and cut them off from the pardon of his death. He forgives the badness of even the worst of us, willy-nilly; and he never takes back that forgiveness, not even at the bottom of the bottomless pit.

The sole difference, therefore, between hell and heaven is that in heaven the forgiveness is accepted and passed along, while in hell it is rejected and blocked. In heaven, the death of the king is welcomed and becomes the doorway to new life in the resurrection. In hell, the old life of the bookkeeping world is insisted on and becomes, forever, the pointless torture it always was.

There is only one unpardonable sin, and that is to withhold pardon from others. The only thing that can keep us out of the joy of the resurrection is to join the unforgiving servant in his refusal to die.

CHAPTER SIX

Losing as Winning

The Prologue to the Good Samaritan

In our study of Jesus' parables up to this point, I have used the Matthean sequence of events and materials as my principal source; now, however, it is time to change guides and follow Luke. The first reason for this change is simply procedural: at the outset, I made a decision to follow the numbering system of the Aland *Synopsis* in establishing the sequence of the parables. To review that sequence briefly, the parables of the kingdom (Aland nos. 122-134—dealt with in a previous volume) all occur within the larger context of Jesus' ministry in Galilee (Aland nos. 30-173.) In addition, the parables of grace we have so far examined in this volume (namely, Aland nos. 144-173) fall into that same, primarily Matthean framework.

But with Aland no. 174 (the decision to go to Jerusalem, Luke 9:51), we begin to follow the predominantly Lukan account of Jesus' leaving Galilee and undertaking his last journey to Jerusalem. Not only does the ensuing collection of materials (which extends all the way to the triumphal entry: Luke 19:28; Aland no. 269) contain the bulk of Jesus' parables of grace, it also shows Jesus "setting his face" to go to Jerusalem. In other words, by the very juxtaposition of sayings and deeds in the Lukan narrative, the rest of the parables of grace are set more and more clearly in the light of Jesus' conviction that his mission will be fulfilled in the mighty act of his dying and rising.

Indeed, it is just that juxtaposition that is the second and substantive reason for the changeover from Matthew to Luke. Up till now, Jesus has mostly *talked*—and talked, as it were, with the clutch of his redeeming death not yet fully engaged. True enough, he has

51

proclaimed a radically left-handed messiahship and he has adumbrated its dark mysteriousness by a constant flow of concepts like lastness, lostness, leastness, littleness, and death. But from now on, it becomes obvious that he is determined to push his insistence on losing-as-winning, on weakness-as-strength, all the way to its logical, *acted-out* conclusion in his own death and resurrection. Accordingly, as we approach the next of the parables of grace (the Good Samaritan: Luke 10:25-37; Aland nos. 182-183), I want to spend a shortish chapter showing how this note of mystery-finally-in-gear manifests itself in Luke's buildup to that parable (Luke 9:51–10:24; Aland nos. 174-181). In particular, I want to demonstrate how, even at this relatively early stage in the final journey to Jerusalem, Jesus himself is already clear that death and resurrection is in fact the key to the operation of grace.

The first passage in this section is a single verse, Luke 9:51. But for all its brevity, it contains not one but two striking references to the mystery of death-resurrection: "And when the days of his being received up *[tas hēméras tēs analēmpseōs autoú]* drew near, he set his face to go to Jerusalem." The noun *análēmpsis* (a taking or receiving up) occurs in the New Testament only at this point. There are, however, nine occurrences of the verb *analambánein* (to take up), five of which (Mark 16:19; Acts 1:2, 11, 22; and 1 Tim. 3:16) refer to Jesus' ascension into heaven. Plainly, then, since Luke is the author of Acts (and uses, in Acts 1:22, practically the same phrase, namely, "the day on which he was taken up"), Luke's allusion to the ascension in the passage at hand is a shorthand way of summing up the entire mystery of death-resurrection that Jesus has come to reveal. Similarly, the "setting of his face toward Jerusalem" has the same mystery as its primary reference. It harks back to Luke's account of the transfiguration (9:30-31), in which Moses and Elijah "appear in glory and speak of [Jesus'] *exodus* that he was about to accomplish at Jerusalem." As Luke handles this one-verse introduction to the last journey to Jerusalem, therefore, it is pregnant with the mystery about to be made manifest. It may have been enough for Matthew (19:1-2) and Mark (10:1) to present the bare details of Jesus' leaving Galilee for Judea. Luke, however, headed as he is for a succession of parables that will positively harp on death-resurrection, cannot let this moment of decision pass without enduing it with the full aura of the mystery.

The next passage we come to (Luke 9:52-56; Aland no. 175) tells of Jesus' rejection by a Samaritan village to which he sent messengers, presumably to make arrangements for a stop during the journey to Jerusalem. "They did not receive him," Luke says, "because he was obviously going toward Jerusalem." Jesus, in other words, having already been rejected by the Jewish authorities because he associated with outcasts (and in particular, with Samaritans—cf. John 4:9), is now rejected by the very outcasts for whom he jeopardized his respectability in the first place.

It is a rerun of the old, disgraceful human story: all of us, even the rankest outsiders, feel better about ourselves if we can keep someone else further outside than we are. The last ethnic group admitted into the volunteer fire department is the very squad that turns, rumps together, horns out, to reject the next group struggling up the social ladder. Jesus came to save a lost and losing world by his own lostness and defeat; but in this wide world of losers, everyone except Jesus remains firmly, if hopelessly, committed to salvation by winning. It hardly matters to us that the victories we fake for ourselves are two-bit victories, or that the losses (and losers) we avoid like the plague are the only vessels in which saving grace comes; we will do anything rather than face either the bankruptcy of our wealth or the richness of our poverty.

And what then is it that we do when we thus disregard our true wealth? We delude ourselves into thinking that our own salvation can be achieved by keeping books on others. The Samaritans wrote Jesus' name down in red ink because he fell short in their religious audit; the Pharisee in Jesus' parable looked down at the publican and thanked God that he himself was not a crook. And we do the same: "I know I'm no prize, but at least I'm better than that lecher, Harry"—as if putting ourselves at the head of a whole column marching in the wrong direction somehow made us less lost than the rest of the troops. It would be funny if it were not fatal; but fatal it is, because grace works only in those who accept their lostness. Jesus came to call sinners, not the pseudo-righteous; he came to raise the dead, not to buy drinks for the marginally alive.

It is not just the Samaritans, though, whose bookkeeping leads them to miss the point of Jesus' determination to go to Jerusalem and death. In Luke 9:54, his disciples James and John turn out to be no better. Even though they have heard everything Jesus has said about lostness—even though they have been the butt of his irony about Gentiles, tax collectors, and other outcasts, and even though they have heard his words to Peter about unlimited forgiveness— they still instinctively resort to salvation by bookkeeping. Confronted with the Samaritan village's rejection of the Jesus they have accepted as the Messiah, the only thing they can think to do is even the score. "Lord," they ask him, "do you want us to bid fire come down from heaven and consume them?" They say in effect, "We're the ones who are winners when it comes to Messiah-watching; let's just get this villageful of losers out of the game with one good, hot blast." Yet they were not winners: they themselves consistently failed to understand Jesus' plain words about his coming death. It would only be much later, after they had seen Jesus himself dead and risen, and after they came to see themselves as dead and risen in him, that they would really be winners. And even at that, most of them would win only by martyrs' deaths—by the very loss, ironically, that they were in such a hurry to inflict on the Samaritans.

But Jesus simply turns and rebukes them (Luke 9:55). The earliest manuscript tradition does not record the substance of the rebuke, but there is a less well-attested tradition that gives it as follows: "And he said, 'You do not know what manner of spirit you are of. For the Son of man did not come to destroy men's lives but to save them.'" In either case, Jesus says a firm no to their whole conception of how the plan of salvation works. He tells them they are talking about something one hundred and eighty degrees opposed to what he himself has in mind. In short, he unceremoniously shuts them up, leaving them with yet another proof that they are losers, and yet another invitation to accept their losing status rather than reject it.

The rest of the Lukan prologue to the parable of the Good Samaritan can be dealt with more briefly; I will note only the points at which it reinforces the thrust of the argument I have been making. In 9:57-62 (Aland no. 176), Jesus effectively throws cold water on three would-be followers. The first of them is apparently an enthusiast who thinks that joining up with Jesus on his journey to Jerusalem will land him unambiguously on a winning team. "I will follow you wherever you go," the man tells Jesus—to which Jesus replies, "Foxes have holes and birds of the air have nests, but the Son of man has nowhere to lay his head." Score another point for Jesus as the divine loser, and for lostness as the touchstone of discipleship.

The second and third characters have a slightly different view of what following Jesus will involve. Number two accepts Jesus' invitation but wants permission first to go and bury his father; number three feels he should be allowed to say a proper good-bye to his family before setting out. To both of them, Jesus says that all such behavior is now irrelevant. "Let the dead bury their own dead," he tells the one, "but as for you, go and proclaim the kingdom of God." And he tells the other, "No one who puts his hand to the plow and looks back is fit for the kingdom of God." In other words, it is not only that the human race's business-as-usual desire to be on the side of a winner is inappropriate to Jesus' mission; it's that *none* of our usual bits of business, however virtuous or proper, has the least bearing on the mystery of redemption. "Follow *me*," he says flatly. "Follow me into my death, because it is only in my death and resurrection that the kingdom comes. All the other tickets to the final, reconciled party—all the moral, philosophical, and religious admission slips on which humanity has always counted—have been cancelled. Nothing counts now except being last, least, lost, little, and dead with me. Buy *that,* and you're home free; buy anything else and you're out in the cold."

And Luke follows up that unvarnished advice with an episode that has even less of a sensible, protective coating on it. In 10:1-12 (Aland no. 177), Jesus appoints seventy others and sends them, two by two, into every town and place where he himself is about to come. "The harvest is plentiful," he tells them, "but the laborers are few" (as well they would be, since no one in his right mind would willingly sign on with a Messiah determined to get himself killed). And as if that weren't enough, he tells them that their own mission will be just as useless: "I send you out as lambs in the midst of wolves" (in other words, as *lost sheep* whose most important credentials will be precisely their lostness and their willingness, in the face of the world's unrelenting wolfishness, to end up as somebody else's dinner). All of which he reinforces by his advice to take no money, no suitcase, no shoes, and to talk to no one on the road. Think of it. He sends them out with no more of the trappings of personal status than a corpse has when it's being shipped home for burial. And when they finally do get to someone's house, they are simply to wish it peace and stay there, eating, drinking, and doing whatever comes along. They are, in short, to be empty vessels, personalities whose contents of initiative and self-determination have been poured down the drain of Jesus' own lostness.

But then (in Luke 10:1-16; Aland nos. 177-179), Jesus drives home the coffin nail of lostness with a series of harsh blows. He tells the seventy (in verses 10-12) that in the entirely likely event that their prospective hosts reject them as freeloading losers, they are simply to shake off the dust of the town against their rejectors and tell them, "Tough luck, winners; you just missed the kingdom of God." Next, he follows that up (in verses 13-15) by pronouncing woes on three of the cities—Chorazin, Bethsaida, and Capernaum—that had just rejected Jesus himself as a loser. And finally (in verse 16), he unequivocally identifies what will happen to them with what has happened and will happen to himself: "He who hears you, hears me" (that is, anyone who accepts your lostness accepts mine), "and he who rejects you rejects me, and he who rejects me rejects him who sent me" (in other words, *losing* is the name of God's game and it's the only game in town: follow *me,* or follow nothing).

In the final verses of this section (Luke 10:17-24; Aland nos. 180-181), the seventy return with joy, saying, "Lord, even the demons are subject to us in your name"—thus missing almost completely the point of the saving emptiness he sent them out to manifest. Jesus—used, by now, to such dunderheadedness—calmly corrects them. "Sure," he says in effect; "I gave you all kinds of power: over snakes and scorpions and over all the power of the enemy. But no matter what you think, kiddies, such right-handed power is not what it's all about. You should be rejoicing only that your names are written in heaven"—which means, if we may push this left-handed, strength-out-of-weakness interpretation all the way to the end of the New Testament, in the *Lamb's book of life,* that is, in the final roster of lost sheep written by none other than the great Lost Sheep Himself.

If that strikes you as an unwarranted extension of Jesus' remarks, consider what comes immediately afterward in verses 21-24. "In that same hour, he rejoiced in the Holy Spirit and said, 'I thank you, Father, Lord of heaven and earth, that you have hidden these things from the wise and understanding and revealed them to babes *[nēpíois]*.'" After all the talk and all the grimness of the journey, Jesus reposes himself in the heart of his mission—in that perfect intimacy he has with the one who sent him—and he sings there of the littleness and the leastness by which the Father wills to reconcile all things to himself. Then finally, turning to the disciples, he says to them privately (even their incomprehension now seeming to him just one more instance of saving lostness), "Blessed are the eyes that see what you see! For I tell you that many prophets and kings desired to see what you see and did not see it, and to hear what you hear and did not hear it."

There is a stunning Latin prayer to St. Joseph that picks up on this text and provides the perfect conclusion to everything I have been trying to say. *"O felicem virum,"* it begins: "O happy man, blessed Joseph, to whom God was given—whom many kings desired to see and did not see, to hear and did not hear—not only to see and to hear, but to carry, to kiss, to clothe, and to care for." Do you grasp the picture? Joseph is the perfect paradigm of our own blessedness. All the things hidden from the wise and understanding (that is, from all the winners who ever lived) are revealed to babes— to the last, the least, the lost, and the little—in the ultimate littleness of God's Holy Child, Jesus himself. Joseph, therefore, is preeminently an empty vessel. A father who, according to tradition, did no begetting, a simple carpenter who understood almost nothing and who died before he could understand more, he ranks now above prophets and kings precisely because, in his own emptiness, he carried, kissed, clothed, and cared for the one who emptied himself for our sakes.

And we are called to do the same. We are not saved by what Jesus taught, and we are certainly not saved by what we understand Jesus to have taught. We are saved by Jesus himself, dead and risen. "Follow *me*," he says. It is the only word that finally matters.

CHAPTER SEVEN

The First of the Misnamed Parables

The Good Samaritan

In its immediate context, the parable of the Good Samaritan (Luke 10:29-37; Aland no. 183) is put forth as Jesus' answer to a question posed by a lawyer (Luke 10:25-28; Aland no. 182). As Luke relates the episode, Jesus is either still in Samaria or perhaps already some distance into Judea; in any case, he is on his way to Jerusalem, and hence to his passion and death. In Matthew and Mark, by contrast, the question is asked in Holy Week, sometime between the triumphal entry and the crucifixion (Matthew has it at 22:34-40, Mark at 12:28-34). In Matthew, it is asked (as in Luke) by a lawyer *(nomikós),* and in Mark, by one of the scribes *(grammatéōn);* only Luke includes the parable of the Good Samaritan as part of Jesus' response.

This difference of placement is of some importance to my interpretation. Holy Week, as far as Jesus' teaching activities were concerned, was the time when he put forth nearly all of his parables of *judgment* as distinct from his parables of *grace.* He was knowingly and deliberately headed for an imminent and unjust death and he found himself engaged in a kind of week-long fencing match with the religious authorities. Their hope was to catch him in some actionable disagreement with the Jewish law; his goal was to provide them with no such grounds—to give them no alternative but to proceed against him illegally. Thus in Matthew, the lawyer tries to trick Jesus (the verb is *peirázein)* into voicing a presumably heterodox view of which commandment in the law was the greatest. In Mark, the scribe (one of the Pharisees) who asks the question has a slightly different and perhaps more kindly program in mind: having just heard Jesus trounce the Sadducees (and thus vindicate the Phar-

58

isees) in an argument about the resurrection at the last day, he seems intent on providing Jesus with an opportunity to make yet another respectably pharisaic pronouncement. In both, however, Jesus simply answers from Scripture, quoting Deut. 6:4-5 and Lev. 19:18. Love of God, he says, is the first and great commandment; love of neighbor, the second. The response is correct, minimal, and above all, cagey.

In Luke, however, Jesus does not answer the question directly. Rather, he maneuvers the lawyer *(nomikós)* into the position of answering it himself and then uses the man's predictably orthodox reply as a springboard into the distinctly unorthodox parable of the Good Samaritan. Jesus, in other words, seems to have a different agenda in Luke than he has in the other two synoptics. He apparently feels no need to be guarded about legalities. Rather, he seems bent on leading the lawyer into an understanding of the themes (namely, lastness, lostness, leastness, littleness, and death) that he has been developing ever since he left Galilee for Jerusalem—which themes, obviously, are the very ones I have chosen to put forth as the interpretative touchstones of all the parables of grace. In summary, therefore, I am about to make as much as I possibly can of Luke's remarkable transposition of the lawyer's question from Holy Week to the Jerusalem journey. There will be little or no *judgment* orientation in what follows here; instead, the *grace* that works by finding the lost and raising the dead will govern all.

The lawyer begins (Luke 10:25) by standing up and addressing Jesus. "Teacher," he says, "what shall I do to inherit eternal life?" Jesus' reply, at least at the outset, seems to be every bit as cagey as his reply in Matthew. In the old rabbinic tradition he turns the question back on the questioner. (I cannot resist paraphrasing Woody Allen's classic formulation of the gambit: *Inquirer:* "Why does a Rabbi always answer a question with a question?" *Rabbi, after a long pause:* "Why *shouldn't* a Rabbi always answer a question with a question?") Accordingly, Jesus asks him, "What is written in the law? How do you interpret it?"

Why does he take this tack? Why is he so guarded at this point in the dialogue, when he will so shortly unburden himself of a parable that is unguardedly offensive in its exaltation of a Samaritan hero over two respectable religious types? I think it is because at the beginning of their exchange he detects a certain hostility in the lawyer's motives. Luke, in fact, gives some support to this view when he introduces the man's question: "Behold, a certain lawyer stood up, putting him to the test" (the verb is *ekpeirázein*). Jesus, of course, has long been aware of the establishment's hostility toward him: as early as Mark 3:6, the Pharisees and the Herodians were trying to figure out a way to destroy him. Hence, when yet another establishment type asks him a religious question, he responds instinctively with caution.

Yet the lawyer's motives were possibly not hostile at all. His question about eternal life may well have been sincere; and in any case, Jesus' reply (including, especially, the parable of the Good Samaritan) certainly seems to respond more to a sincere interest than to an implied threat. But what exactly was that interest? On what basis could an expert in the Torah have come to think that Jesus might actually have something religiously important to say? Well, perhaps on the basis of his having heard Jesus' recent and mysterious exaltation of losing over winning, of being last instead of first. Perhaps he overheard Jesus' remarks to would-be followers (Luke 9:57-62)—or possibly, his prayer of rejoicing in the Holy Spirit (Luke 10:21) in which he thanked the Father that he had "hid these things from the wise and understanding and revealed them to babes." Admittedly, Luke does not easily give up his own suspicions: even after the lawyer has answered his own question by quoting the summary of the deuteronomic and levitical law—and even after Jesus has given him a peaceable pat on the back ("You have answered correctly; do this and you will live")—Luke still prefaces the lawyer's next question ("And who is my neighbor?") with the hostile comment, "But he, wanting to justify himself. . . ."

In any case, by the time Jesus actually starts addressing the question of neighbor in the parable of the Good Samaritan, he himself seems definitely to have dropped his guard. As I read him, he has decided to deal unsuspiciously, if provocatively, with what he takes to be a mind honestly curious about the mystery of lostness. Needless to say, other interpretations of this sequence are possible. But what convinces me of the validity of the one I am making is the content of the parable itself: the Good Samaritan is a veritable paean to lostness, outcastness, and even, in a certain sense, death.

I suppose I had best lay my cards face up right here. To me, the central figure in the parable is not the Samaritan. He is simply one of the three characters in the story who have the opportunity to display neighborliness as Jesus defines it. The defining character—the one to whom the other three respond by being non-neighbor or neighbor—is the man who fell among thieves. The actual Christ-figure in the story, therefore, is yet another loser, yet another down-and-outer who, by just lying there in his lostness and proximity to death (*hēmithanē,* "practically dead," is the way Jesus describes him), is in fact the closest thing to Jesus in the parable.

That runs counter, of course, to the better part of two thousand years' worth of interpretation, but I shall insist on it. This parable, like so many of Jesus' most telling ones, has been egregiously misnamed. It is not primarily about the Samaritan but about the man on the ground (just as the Prodigal Son is not about a boy's sins but about his father's forgiveness, and just as the Laborers in the Vineyard is not about the workers but about the beneficent vineyard-owner). This means, incidentally, that Good Samaritan Hospitals have been likewise misnamed. It is the suffering, dying patients in such institutions who look most like Jesus in his redeeming work, not the doctors with their authoritarian stethoscopes around their necks. Accordingly, it would have been much less misleading to have named them Man-Who-Fell-Among-Thieves Hospitals. But then the medical profession might sense libel in such an attempt at theological correctness. Back to my argument.

What I am most concerned to skewer at this point is precisely the theological mischief caused by the misnaming of this parable. Calling it the Good Samaritan inevitably sets up its hearers to take it as a story whose hero offers them a good example for imitation. I am, of course, aware of the fact that Jesus ends the parable precisely on the note of imitation: "You, too, go and do likewise." But the common, good-works interpretation of the imitation to which Jesus invites us all too easily gives the Gospel a fast shuffle. True enough, we are called to imitation. But imitation of what, exactly? Is it not the *imitatio Christi,* the following of Jesus? And is not that following of him far more than just a matter of doing kind acts? Is it not the following of him into the only mystery that can save the world, namely, his passion, death, and resurrection? Is it not, *tout court,* the taking up of his cross?

Therefore, if you want to say that the parable of the Good Samaritan tells us to imitate the Samaritan in his sharing of the passion and near-death of the man who fell among thieves—if you want to read his selfless actions as so many ways in which he took the outcastness and lostness of the Christ-figure on the ground into his own outcast and losing life—then I will let you have imitation as one of the main themes of the parable. But please note that such an interpretation is not at all what people generally have in mind when the subject of imitating the Good Samaritan is broached to them. What their minds instantly go to is something quite different, something that is utterly destructive of the notion of a grace that works only by death and resurrection. Because what they imagine themselves called upon to imitate is not a mystery of lostness and death graspable only by left-handed faith; rather, it is a mere plausibility—a sensible if slightly heroic career of successful care-giving based on the performance of right-handed good works.

What is wrong with that? Quite simply, it blows the Good News right out of the water. For if the world could have been saved by providing good examples to which we could respond with appropriately good works, it would have been saved an hour and twenty minutes after Moses came down from Mt. Sinai. "For if there had been a law given which could have given life, verily righteousness should have been by the law. But the scripture hath concluded all under sin, that the promise by faith of Jesus Christ might be given to them that believe" (Gal. 3:21-22, KJV). Do you see the problem? Salvation is not some felicitous state to which we can lift ourselves by our own bootstraps after the contemplation of sufficiently good examples. It is an utterly new creation into which we are brought by our death in Jesus' death and our resurrection in his. It comes not out of our own efforts, however well-inspired or successfully pursued, but out of the shipwreck of all human effort whatsoever. And therefore if there is any ministering to be imitated in the Good Samaritan's example, it is the ministry to Jesus in his passion, as that passion is to be found in the least of his brethren, namely, in the hungry, the thirsty, the outcast, the naked, the sick, and the imprisoned in whom he dwells and through whom he invites us to become his neighbors in death and resurrection (see the parable of the Great Judgment, Matt. 25:31-46).

But that dark invitation is so far removed from the glittering generality of salvation by imitating good examples that I think now, perhaps, you can begin to see what I am getting at. Neither the

Samaritan nor, a fortiori, Jesus is an example of some broader, saving truth about the power of human niceness. Jesus is an example of nothing of the sort. He is the incarnation of the unique, saving mystery of death and resurrection. We do not move from him to some deeper reality called love or goodness that will finally do the trick and make the world go round. No human virtues, however exalted or assiduously practiced, will ever make that cut. Love, as we so regularly mismanage it, is the largest single factor in making our personal worlds go down the drain: psychiatrists' couches are not kept warm by patients complaining of the depredations of total strangers. And goodness, as we so self-interestedly define it, is the mainspring of all the really great evils of the world. The extermination of six million Jews, for example, was done precisely in the name of a perverse vision of goodness—of a totally Aryan society that would bring in the millennium just as soon as the non-Aryans were weeded out. Rather, we move from the disasters of our loving and the bankruptcies of our goodness into the passion of Jesus where alone we can be saved. Niceness has nothing to do with the price of our salvation.

Besides, as everyone knows, nice guys finish last. Good Samaritans are sued with alarming regularity; and if one of them does manage to stay out of court, he probably goes home and loses all the benefits of his goodness in a fight with his wife over putting some deadbeat's expenses on Visa. Scripture hath concluded—locked up—*all* under sin. The entail of our sinfulness cannot be broken by good examples, even if, *per impossible*, we could follow them. Quite the contrary, the Gospel says clearly that we can be saved only by bad examples: by the stupid example of a Samaritan who spends his livelihood on a loser, and by the horrible example of a Savior who, in an excruciating death, lays down his life for his friends.

Give me that and I will let you have the Good Samaritan as a model for behavior. But example me no nicer examples. The troops have been confused enough for two thousand years. We don't need even another minute's worth of sermons about good works. On to the parable, then, for a look at its details through fresh eyes.

"A certain man," Jesus says, "went down from Jerusalem to Jericho." Consider first the physical remarkability of the journey. It is downhill all the way. Jerusalem stands 2,500 feet above the level of the Mediterranean and Jericho lies 825 feet below it. That's a drop of the better part of three-fifths of a mile and it takes the man in question down into increasingly depressing territory. Without making too much of it, I am disposed to take Jesus' postulation of such a descent as a parable in itself of his own downhill journey to his passion and death, and thus into the lastness, lostness, etc., that he now sees as the heart of his saving work. And as if to underscore the allusion, he adds a whole string of details that mark the man as a loser par excellence: "he fell among thieves who stripped him and beat him up and went away, leaving him half dead." Score several points for my notion that the man who fell among thieves is the authentic Christ-figure in the parable of the Good Samaritan.

"By chance," Jesus continues, "a certain priest was going down that road and when he saw the man, he passed by on the other side." So too, Jesus says, did a Levite when he came to the place. Note the nature of these first two candidates for the possible role of neighbor to the unfortunate who is this parable's surrogate for the Messiah. Jesus is talking, of course, to a lawyer, an interpreter of the Torah; but the people he adduces at this point do not exactly correspond to the lawyer. True enough, they owe their respective callings to the Torah; but they are far less involved in interpreting it than they are in offering the temple sacrifices it enjoins. Jesus' reference here, therefore, may well be at least a glancing one to the whole sacrificial system conceived of as an instrument of salvation. Consider the picture: two official representatives of atonement as understood by the religious authorities of Jesus' day find themselves unable or unwilling to see a wounded loser as having any claim on their attention or any relevance to their work. In short, they think of themselves as winners. They have all their vocational ducks in a row and they see no point in allowing either their lives or their spiritual, moral, or physical plans for the season to be ruined by attention to some outcast. How like the reaction Jesus himself received! He came to his own country and his own people did not receive him (John 1:11). He was despised and rejected (Isa. 53:3) for dying as a common criminal. He himself, in other words, was as unrecognizable a Christ-figure as the man who fell among thieves. Admittedly, it was eventually claimed of him that on the third day he rose from the dead. But rising from the dead was a totally insufficient apology for the abysmally bad messianic taste he had shown by dying in the first place. Real Messiahs don't die.

Finally, though, Jesus brings on the Good Samaritan. Note once again the nature of the character introduced as the man of the hour: he is an outcast come to deal with an outcast, a loser come to minister to another loser. The man who fell among thieves presumably was a Jew; therefore, if either the priest or the Levite had bothered to make his acquaintance, they would have recognized him as one of their own. But since the shipwreck of his life had made him unrecognizable to them, he might as well (as might Jesus in his dereliction, please note) not have been a Jew at all. He, like Jesus, seemed only reproachable. They could not bring themselves to go forth out of their safe theological and psychological camp to meet him and bear his reproach (Heb. 13:13).

But the Samaritan, already under reproach himself (cf. John 4:9), has no such problem. Instead, he goes to the man on the ground—the surrogate for the Savior—and he involves himself in his passion. He binds up his wounds, pouring in oil and wine—all acts of kindness, to be sure, but also acts that any normal person would find inconveniencing, distasteful, and depriving, not to mention expensive of both time and resources. Moreover, he puts the man on his own animal, thus effectively dying to his own comfort and to whatever prospects he may have had of accomplishing his journey in good time. Next, he brings him to an inn and takes care of him for the whole night, further interrupting his own progress and frustrating his travelling man's dearest wish, namely, a peaceful Scotch in the motel bar and an early, quiet bed after a hard day on the road. And as if all that weren't enough, he gets up in the morning, goes down to the front desk, and books the mugging victim in for an indefinite stay, all expenses paid—room, meals, doctors, nurses, medicines, health club, and limo if needed—and no questions asked. To sum it up, he lays down a very good approximation of his life for someone who isn't even his friend, simply because he, as an outcast, finally has found someone who lives in his own neighborhood, namely, the place where the discards of respectable religiosity are burned outside the camp (again, Heb. 13:11-13)—the dump, in other words, to which are consigned the last, the lost, the least, the little, and the dead.

And having said all that, Jesus invites the lawyer to answer his own question. "Which one of these three," he asks, "seems to you to have been a neighbor to the one who fell among thieves?" It is a setup, of course, and the lawyer gives the only possible reply: "He who showed kindness to him"—which leads Jesus to the punch line of the parable, "You go and do the same."

As I said, I take that to be light-years away from an exhortation to general human niceness. Jesus' whole parable, especially with its piling up of detail after detail of extreme, even irrational, behavior on the part of the Samaritan, points not to meritorious exercises of good will but to the sharing of the passion as the main thrust of the story. What is to be imitated in the Samaritan's action is not his moral uprightness in doing good deeds but his spiritual insight into the truly bizarre working of the mystery of redemption. The lawyer is told by Jesus, in effect, to stop trying to live and to be willing to die, to be willing to be lost rather than to be found—to be, in short, a neighbor to the One who, in the least of his brethren, is already neighbor to the whole world of losers.

As if to underscore the validity of this interpretation, Luke concludes the tenth chapter of his Gospel (in verses 38-42) with the story of Jesus' visit to Mary and Martha—which, if I may use a musical illustration, I take to be a coda to what Jesus has just said in the parable of the Good Samaritan about the centrality of his passion to the whole question of life eternal, and even of life here and now.

Jesus goes into a village and a woman named Martha welcomes him. Martha brings him to her house and immediately gets her nose out of joint because her sister Mary just sits at Jesus' feet and rapturously soaks up every word he says. Finally, when Martha has had all she can take of her sister's calf-eyed preoccupation with Jesus, she simply loses it right in front of everybody. "Lord," she says, "don't you care that my sister has left me to do all the work by myself? Tell her to help me!" Martha's problem is that, for all her welcoming of Jesus, she is just too busy (as the priest and the Levite were too busy) with her own life to pay impractical attention to somebody who isn't about to give her the kind of help she thinks she needs. She has carefully kept her life's books and, like all bookkeepers when their stock in trade is denigrated, she can only lash out with a tirade of blame (aimed at Jesus as well as her sister) against the unproductiveness of just hanging around.

But Jesus (who, as we believe, saves us precisely by just hanging around) puts her—and all the bookkeepers, and all the other captains of their souls and masters of their fates—out of business with the lesson of the Good Samaritan all over again. "Martha, Martha," he says, "you get worried and worked up about so many things. It's a wonder you don't kill yourself with all the effort it's taking you to hold your life together. Let it go. As long as the most important thing in your life is to keep finding your way, you're going to live in mortal terror of losing it. Once you're willing to be lost, though, you'll be home free. Your lostness is the one thing no one will ever be able to take away from you. The only ticket anybody needs is the one ticket everybody already has, and Mary, like the Samaritan, has chosen to use it. Come on. Sit down and let's get lost together."

CHAPTER EIGHT

Grace More Than Judgment

From the Friend at Midnight to the Rich Fool

The next group of parables in the Lukan sequence runs from 11:1 to 12:21 (Aland nos. 185-200). This section comprises not only two parables generally recognized as such (the Friend at Midnight and the Rich Fool), but also a welter of less formal parabolic teachings and sayings (the kingdom divided against itself, the return of the unclean spirit, the sign of Jonah, the light of the body, the leaven of the Pharisees, the five sparrows, and the hairs of the head).

Even though there is a judgmental aspect to many of these utterances, I shall remain true to my plan of attack and read them primarily as parables of grace. Admittedly, two of the items in this section (the denunciation of the Pharisees and scribes, and the Watchful Servants) are placed by Matthew in Holy Week—where, by my analysis, they are properly parables of judgment. But the rest of this material—in Matthew and Mark as well as in Luke—occurs before the triumphal entry and, accordingly, justifies my insistence that it should all be read in the light of Jesus' final journey to Jerusalem. He is going to his death: therefore death and resurrection must continue to be regarded as the clockwork, so to speak, that makes his parables of grace tick.

Jesus begins these sayings (at Luke 11:1) with the Lord's Prayer, and he segues immediately into the parable of the Friend at Midnight. Take the Lord's Prayer first. As Luke gives it, it is Jesus' response to a request that he should, like John the Baptist, teach his disciples to pray. Furthermore, the Lukan version of the prayer—especially as most modern editors of the text now read it—is far shorter (38 words as against 57 in the Greek) than the one in Matt. 6.

When I put those two facts together, they suggest to me that Jesus' intention in giving such a short prayer is to accede to the request while at the same time denying it, or at least holding up a warning hand against the implied equation of his ministry with that of John the Baptist. As I observed above in chapter two, Jesus has already distanced himself considerably from the program of salvation as envisioned by John. Redemption as the Baptist proclaimed it was largely a matter of placing oneself in a position of ethical, religious, and political uprightness so that membership in the coming kingdom could be insured. As Jesus envisions it, however, inclusion in the kingdom has already happened—and happened for everyone—in the catholic mystery of which he himself is the sacramental embodiment (see my first volume, *The Parables of the Kingdom*, e.g., the Growing Seed, the Yeast, etc.). Furthermore, as Jesus proclaims this mystery on his way to Jerusalem, it calls not for triumphant, upright action but simply for being last, lost, least, little, and dead—all of which, luckily, everyone eventually will be, willy-nilly. In short, it is a gift already given to the world in its dereliction, not a plausibility to be negotiated for with a down payment of good deeds.

Therefore when Jesus is asked to match John the Baptist's programmatic performance on the subject of prayer, he draws back. His disciples want religious training and spiritual formation. But Jesus, apparently convinced by now that no human achievements, either religious or moral, can bring in the kingdom, gives only the barest bones of a prayer. In fact, he gives one in which the only human action held up for imitation is forgiveness—an act that is inevitably linked, in plain human terms as well as in terms of Jesus' eventual ministry, with a willingness to be dead.

I realize that this sounds as if I am assigning Paul's theology to Jesus' consciousness. I am and I am not. I do not think, of course, that Jesus had Paul's categories as such in mind. But I do think that on any serious view of either the inspiration of Scripture or the history of salvation as spelled out in Scripture, the risen and ascended Jesus hired Paul on the road to Damascus precisely for the job of rescuing his essential teaching from misunderstanding. There were far too many in the early church (notably, the authorities of the Jerusalem church) who felt themselves called to peddle the exact opposite of what Jesus had in mind. To them, law—or as we might put it more broadly, religion—was a precondition of acceptance into the fellowship of the Gospel. Therefore it was left to Paul—who saw clearly that only faith in the dead and risen Jesus was necessary to salvation—to oppose that view and thus to become the ultimate scriptural guide to Jesus' teaching. I like to imagine that what Jesus actually said to Paul on the Damascus road was not, "Saul, Saul, why do you persecute me?" but, "Help! I'm a prisoner in a commandment factory." The emendation is a bit of whimsy, of course. But it does underscore the fact that Paul was called to articulate, in other and later words, the very thing that Jesus had been saying earlier and in his own way.

In any case, the Lord's Prayer, which is clearly a preface to the parable of the Friend at Midnight, is exceedingly odd in its content, in its proportions, and in its adequacy as a response to a request for a religious formula. It begins, simply, "Father"—an opening that to me speaks not of someone with whom we will have a relationship after certain pious or ethical exercises but of the One to whom we are already related by sonship. More than that, it suggests that for both the disciples and us, the sonship we have is precisely Jesus' own—that we stand before the Father *in him* (*"in the beloved,"* Eph. 1:6, to use the Pauline phraseology). We pray, in other words, not out of our own dubious supplicative competencies but in the power of his death and resurrection. Or to put it most correctly, he (and the Spirit as well) *prays in us.* Prayer is not really our work at all.

Then, after no more than a "hallowed be your name" and a "let your kingdom come," he tells them to pray for nothing more by way of human achievement than the food they need day by day. No spiritual attainments, no ethical perfections; just the bare necessities to keep body and soul together so they can get on, presumably, with the one thing really necessary, namely, that "good part"—that quiet union with himself in his death and resurrection—which, just three verses earlier, he chided Martha for derogating in her sister Mary.

And that leads him into the heart of the prayer, the longest single topic in its brief contents. "Forgive us our sins as we forgive every one who is indebted to us." The Gospel truth is that forgiveness comes to us because God in Jesus died to and for our sins—because, in other words, the Shepherd himself became a lost sheep for our sake. And it is just that truth, I think, that Jesus underscores when he holds up the forgiveness of debts as the model for our imitation of his forgiving. A person who cancels a debt is a person who dies to his own rightful possession of life. Unless he does it out of mindlessness or idiotic calculation, he cannot write off what is justly due him without accepting his own status as a loser, that is, *as dead*. Death and resurrection are the key to the whole mystery of our redemption. We pray in Jesus' death and resurrection, we are forgiven in Jesus' death and resurrection, and we forgive others in Jesus' death and resurrection. If we attempt any of those things *while still trying to preserve our life,* we will never manage them. They are possible only because we are dead and our life is hid with Christ in God (Col. 3:3). And they can be celebrated by us only if we accept death as the vehicle of our life in him.

It is just this insistence, as I see it, that leads Jesus to the last phrase of the prayer, "and do not lead us into trial *[peirasmón]*." Life is a web of trials and temptations, but only one of them can ever be fatal, and that is the temptation to think it is by further, better, and more aggressive living that we can have life. But that will never work. If the world could have lived its way to salvation, it would have, long ago. The fact is that it can only *die* its way there, *lose* its way there. The precise temptation, therefore, into which we pray we will not be led is the temptation to reject our saving death and try to proceed on our living own. Like the blasphemy against the Holy Spirit, that is the one thing that cannot be forgiven, precisely because it is the refusal of the only box in which forgiveness is ever delivered.

All of which, for Luke, leads directly into the parable of the Importunate Friend at Midnight. Jesus asks the disciples to suppose that they have a friend who is home in bed at midnight. Note what that means. He has them posit, as the figure of God the Father in this parable, a person who is deep in the experience of the nearest ordinary sacrament of death available to living people, namely, the daily expiration of falling asleep—that radically uncontrollable, lost state in which all reasonable responses to life are suspended. Next, he invites them to imagine that they break in upon that parabolic death of God with a veritable battering ram of reasonable requests. He gives them a whole rigamarole of plausible arguments with which to persuade their dead friend to rise. They need three loaves; they need them so they can feed a ravenously hungry guest; and they could not have come any sooner because their guest has only just now arrived. They would, of course, have raided their own pantry, but alas, this was not their day to go food shopping and they are fresh out of everything. The sleeper is their only hope.

Astonishingly, though, Jesus has the surrogate for God give them the cold shoulder. The sleeper's first response is a not-really-awake "don't bother me," followed by a more organized list of reasons for them to get lost: "The door is already locked, my children are with me in the bed, and I can't get up to give you anything" (Luke 11:7).

Time for a halt. My reading of death and resurrection into this text may make you suspect that I am guilty of charley-horsing the arm of Scripture. I am not. Consider the evidence. The Greek for "I am not able to get up to give you anything" is *ou dýnamai anastás doúnai soi*. The word *anastás* is from *anistánai* (to raise, to rise), which, along with the verb *egeírein* (to raise, to rouse), is one of the two major roots used in the New Testament to refer to resurrection. Moreover, this is not the only use of resurrection language in this parable: *anastás* appears again in verse 8, as does *egertheís*. This parable tells us, therefore, that it is out of death, not out of life, that God rises to answer our prayers. And note well that he rises not in response to the reasonableness (or the moral uprightness) of our requests but *for no good reason other than to raise the rest of the dead*.

Look at the way Jesus actually puts it (Luke 11:8): "I tell you, even if he will not get up *[anastás]* and give you the bread because he is your friend, yet on account of your shamelessness *[anaídeian]* he will rise *[egertheís]* and give you as much as you need." What is this shamelessness but death to self? People who lead reasonable, respectable lives—who are preoccupied first and foremost with the endless struggle to think well of themselves—do not obtrude upon their friends' privacy at midnight. And why don't they? Because that would display them as thoughtless beggars and make them look bad. But if someone were dead to all that—if he could come to his friend's house with nothing more than the confession that he was a total loss as a host (or anything else)—then precisely because of his shamelessness, his total lack of a self-regarding life, he would be raised out of that death by his rising friend.

I am aware that the usual interpretation of this passage renders *anaídeian* as "shameless persistence" and then goes on to maintain that if we nag God enough, he will come through with the wherewithal for our lives. I have nothing against urging persistence in prayer; but I do think that holding it up as the main point of this particular parable gives, if not a charley horse, then at least an Indian burn to the arm of Scripture. Note that Jesus carefully avoids crediting any of the *content* of the importunate friend's request with efficacy. His reasons, his carefully argued justifications for asking his friend to rise and give him bread, are all sloughed off with a peremptory "I'm dead; go away." To hold, then, that Jesus is telling us that God will rise to our help simply because we go on repeating the same arguments seems to me not only unwarranted here but also perilously contrary to his words in Matt. 6:7, "When you pray, do not use a lot of words [*mē battalogēsēte*—don't babble, don't use 'vain repetition'], as the pagans do, who think they will be heard because of their much speaking [*polylogía*]."

No, God rises from his death in Jesus not to satisfy our requests, reasonable or unreasonable, unexpressed or overexpressed, but to raise us from our own deaths. All we need to offer in order to share in the joy of his rising is the shameless, selfless admission that we are dead without him, and the faith to confess that we are also dead with him and in him. The whole parable, therefore, is a conjugation of prayer according to the paradigm of death and resurrection—a footnote to the Lord's Prayer, if you will, in which Jesus tells us that even the daily bread he taught us to pray for comes only out of death. And the rest of the passage (Luke 11:9-13) is more of the same.

Once again, I am aware of the more usual "persistence wins" interpretation given to lines like "Ask and it will be given to you, seek and you will find, knock and it will be opened to you" (Luke 11:9ff.). But in fact, persistence doesn't win anywhere near often enough to be held up as the precondition of God's answering prayer. And I will not let you hand me the cheap, cruel bromide that when persistence doesn't win it probably wasn't real persistence. Tell that to somebody who asked, and sought, and knocked till her knuckles bled for a child who eventually died of leukemia anyway. Or if you don't have the nerve for that, try at least to remember that no matter how persistent or productive your prayers, there will inevitably be, on some dark day, one whoppingly unproductive prayer of yours (the prayer to be spared your death just one more time) that God will answer, "Sorry; the door of your life is already shut; all my real children are with me in the bed of my death; and I'm not about to rise from the dead just to give you back the same old two-bit life you were perishing of. Bring me a shameless acceptance of your death, though, and I'll show you how I really do business."

It is in that light, therefore, that we should look at the last part of the text. "Everyone who asks, receives," Jesus says, "and he who seeks, finds, and to him who knocks, it will be opened." Taken literally as a program for conning God into catering to the needs of our lives, that is pure bunk: too many sincere, persistent prayers have simply gone unfulfilled. But taken as a command constantly to bring our deaths to his death and to find our resurrection in his, it is solid gold. Furthermore, consider the clincher that Jesus adds: "What father among you will give his son a snake when he asks for a fish, or a scorpion when he asks for an egg? If you then, *being evil [ponēroí],* know how to give good gifts to your children, how much more will the heavenly Father give *the Holy Spirit* to those who ask him?"

The two italicized phrases sum up my case. "If you then, *being evil. . . .*" "If you," Jesus seems to be saying, "—you who can never manage to be anything more than reasonable, who can make only fallen, sinful sense, and who are trapped in a losing battle to make a radically uncooperative world say uncle—if you whose best is none too good can still care enough to provide kippers and eggs for the condemned—how much more will the heavenly Father give you resurrection from your lifelong death?" For it is precisely resurrection that the Father and the Son have appointed as the principal gift of the Holy Spirit. Listen to Jesus in John. "But when he, the Spirit of truth comes, he will lead you into all truth. He will not speak of himself [*pace* all the self-appointed Spirit promoters], but whatever he hears he will speak, and he will proclaim to you things to come. He will glorify *me,* for he will take *of mine* and proclaim it to you" (John 16:13-14). The work of the Spirit is nothing other than the work of Jesus; and the work of Jesus is the raising of the dead.

This Lukan passage on prayer, then, far from being a pious sop—far from being a promise of spiritual comfort to make up for an inveterate failure to deliver material gifts, whether in full, on time, or at all—this conclusion to the parable of the Friend at Midnight is nothing less than a proclamation of the heart of the Good News. We have died. We do not have to ask for death, or seek it, or work ourselves up to it. We have only to accept the death we already have, and in the clean emptiness of that death we will find the life that all along has been hid for us with Christ in God (Col. 3:3). We are safe, not because of the reasonableness or persistence of our prayers but because he lives in our death. Entombed together with him in baptism, we have already been raised up together in him through faith in the working of God who raised him from the dead (Col. 2:12). While we were dead in our trespasses, he made us alive together in Christ—by *grace* we are saved—and he raised us up together and made us sit together in the heavenly places in Christ Jesus (Eph. 2:5, 6). And all of that *now*. Not just hereafter, and certainly not just a week from some Tuesday.

That, in the last analysis, is why we pray. Not to get some reasonable, small-bore job done, but to celebrate the job beyond all liking and happening that has already been done for us and in us by Jesus. We have a friend in our death; in the end, he meets us nowhere else. Prayer is the flogging of the only Dead Horse actually able to rise.

The next passage in this sequence (Luke 11:14-26; Aland nos. 188-189) deals with Jesus' response (after he had given speech to a dumb man who was possessed) to the charge that he cast out demons by Beelzebul, the prince of the demons. His parabolic retort ("Every kingdom divided against itself is laid waste, etc.") seems at first to be saying little more than, "If the devil is behind this, how come he's fighting against himself?" But what Jesus really seems to be getting at, once again, is the inability of the world to straighten itself up by any kind of reasonable, sensible action, human *or* angelic. "If you're going to play that Beelzebul game," he says in effect, "all you'll ever succeed in doing is discrediting even the minor cures you yourselves are able to perform. But if it is by *the finger of God* that I cast out demons, then the kingdom of God has come upon you."

The Finger of God. In the church fathers—and most notably in the great Latin hymn, *Veni Creator Spiritus* ("Come Holy Ghost")— the phrase is taken as one of the titles of the Holy Spirit.

> *Tu septiformis munere,*
> *dextrae Dei tu digitus*
> *tu rite promisso patris*
> *sermone dittans guttura.*

The sevenfold gifts of grace are thine,
O finger of the Hand Divine;
True promise of the Father thou,
Who dost the tongue with speech endow.

(Stanza 3, Hymnal 1940 translation)

Dextrae Dei Digitus, the Finger of the *right* hand of God. In a previous volume, *The Parables of the Kingdom,* I took the liberty of indulging myself in a theological lark. I pointed out that in both Greek and Latin, the ordinary way of saying "right hand" is simply to use the word "right," omitting any actual mention of "hand." I did that in order to suggest that when Jesus ascends and sits *ek dexión tou patrós* (on the right of the Father), it might just be possible to think of him as ruling, not by virtue of the unparadoxical, straight-line power of the right *hand* of God but out of the right *side* of God's brain. That only substituted one analogical formulation for another; but as we now understand the functioning of the brain, it is precisely the right hemisphere that governs the left hand—and it is by the paradoxical, indirect power of God's left hand that he saves the world in the death and resurrection of Jesus. I take the same liberty now.

It is by the Holy Spirit, the presiding genius of the Gospel—the one who takes of the left-handed work of Jesus and shows it to us—that Jesus does what he does. And what he does is *raise the dead.* His power is not from this plausible, perishing world, nor is it from the prince of this hopelessly divided kingdom. It is from himself in the death and resurrection by which alone the true kingdom comes. "The world," he says in effect (Luke 11:21ff.), "is full of strong-arm, right-handed types; but when the stronger, left-handed arm comes, it takes away all the armor in which the world trusted and divides the spoils of its plausible efforts. He who is not with me, therefore, is against me; and he who does not gather with me [in the field of my death, and there only] scatters." And then, in a solemn warning, he sums up his case: "When the unclean spirit [which I take to mean the plausible spirit of right-handed action] has gone out of a man, it travels through waterless places looking for a place to rest, but it doesn't find one."

Think about that. We have seen, perhaps, the light of the Gospel. We have realized that it is in our lastness, lostness, leastness, littleness, and death—and not in the chewing-gum and baling-wire contraptions of our lives—that we are saved. But that left-handed truth is hard to hold onto, and so by and by, when the unclean spirit returns, it finds us empty, swept, and put in order by the new broom of Jesus' death. And what does it do? It goes and brings seven other spirits more evil than mere right-handed action: it finds ways of standing the Gospel itself on its head. It takes prayer—prayer that was meant to be a standing in Jesus' death—and turns it into right-handed spiritual exercises. It takes forgiveness of sins—forgiveness that can come only by death and resurrection—and turns it into a reward for plausible, convincing repentance. It takes, in short, the grace of God that works by raising the dead and converts it into a transaction available only to those with acceptable lives. And so seven—or seven hundred—spirits enter and dwell in us, and our last state is worse than the first.

It is the old, sad story of the errant tendencies of doctrine-producing minds. The saving truth has been gladly found, and then disastrously lost, over and over and over. In spite of it all, though, Jesus' power does not come through anything here except death. Unless we can be content to sit quietly in that clean, empty room, all the evils of the world will come, tracking their reasonable, hopeless grime back in. Our strength, like the strength of the Stronger One who saved us, is literally to sit still.

But you are fidgeting. "If that isn't an out-and-out charley-horsing of Scripture," you say, "I've never seen one." Well, perhaps it is. I make no apologies. On with the text.

Hearing all this from Jesus, a woman in the crowd speaks up and says to him (Luke 11:27, 28), "Blessed is the womb that bore you and the breasts that you sucked." Jesus' mother, she suggests—with all the enthusiasm of a mind that, along with the church, has missed nearly the whole point of his words on this journey to Jerusalem and death—must be very proud of her son's snappy performance. To which Jesus replies, "No; blessed are those who hear the word of God and keep it." If the Blessed Virgin Mary had any blessedness, it showed itself not in babble about "my son, the wonder-working rabbi," but in her own hearing and keeping of the word of his passion and death. She is (credit the church with having gotten at least this much right about her) the *mater dolorosa,* the sorrowful mother. Through her entire life, she was pierced with the sword prophesied by Simeon (Luke 2:35). Her child, as Simeon said in the temple, "was put here for the fall [*ptōsin*—the variant, *ptōma,* means corpse] and the rising [*anástasin*—resurrection, yet again] of many in Israel, and for a sign that will be spoken against." Mary is thus the first fruit of him who is the firstfruits of them that slept.

Which brings us nicely to the next passage, the Sign of Jonah (Luke 11:29-32; Aland no. 191). The crowds on the journey are getting bigger, but Jesus is not happy about them. "This generation is an evil [*ponērá*] generation," he says. "They seek a sign, but no sign will be given to them except the sign of Jonah." Not so oddly, from my point of view, he uses here the same word, "evil," that he used only a little while ago to describe us when we answer our children's prayers ("If you then, being evil . . ."). I say not oddly, because he is making the same point, contrasting the world's plausible, right-handed way of giving help with God's mysterious, left-handed program of salvation by raising the dead. He knows they have not heard what he is saying, let alone understood what he is proposing to do. But he spells it out for them anyway: *no signs.* No divine responses to ethical probity, religious correctness, or spiritual competency. Only the sign of Jonah, which Matthew (12:40ff.) gives in so many words: "As Jonah was in the belly of the whale three days and three nights, so the Son of man will be three days and three nights in the heart of the earth." He will offer them, as the sign of the mystery of faith, only his resurrection from the dead. "The men of Nineveh," he tells them, "will arise [*anastḗsontai*] at the judgment with this generation and condemn it." (The entire human race rises in Jesus, please note; but those of us who reject the death out of which resurrection comes will hardly accept our rising.) "And they will condemn it," Jesus continues, "because they repented at the preaching of Jonah, and behold, a greater than Jonah is here." So, too, Jesus says, with the Queen of Sheba, because she came from the ends of the earth to hear the wisdom of Solomon, and behold, a greater than Solomon is here.

In the resurrection, we shall finally see that all the signs we asked for in our plausible, evil minds pale into insignificance before the sign actually given. The world is not saved because of its repentance, its wisdom, or its goodness—and certainly not because of its stumbling efforts to become either sorrier, wiser, or better. Rather it is saved because it is a dead world, and because the life of him who is greater than Jonah or Solomon has reigned out of its death. We have always been safe in our deaths. It's just that, until Jesus, we could never see them as the sign of our salvation.

The rest of the parabolic passages in this section can be read partly as comments on that truth, partly as prologue to the parable of the Rich Fool, and partly as a coda to the whole composition. Let me enter them into the record briefly.

In Luke 11:33-36 (Aland nos. 192-193), Jesus says, "No one lights a lamp and then hides it or puts it under a bucket; rather, he puts it on the lampstand that those who enter may see the light." He is speaking principally, I take it, of himself: the light he will not hide is the mystery of his death and resurrection. And he presses the comparison. "Your eye," he says, "is the lamp of your body: when your eye is sound [*haploús:* single, or simple; sometimes, in a pejorative sense, silly; also, clear, doing only what it is supposed to do], your whole body will be full of light [that is, full of the benefits of the eye's single-minded pursuit of light instead of darkness]. But when it is evil [*ponērós*] your body will be full of darkness. Watch therefore lest the light that is in you be darkness. If then your whole body be light, having no part [*méros*] dark, it will be bright all over, as when a lamp shines on you with its light."

Once again, Jesus brings in the word *ponērós*, "evil." And once again, he uses it to stand for the pursuit of all those plausible schemes by which we try unsuccessfully to make our lives come out even. Sadly, though, our bright ideas turn out to be only dim bulbs: our frantic living does not produce life. But if we allow the devastatingly simple, single truth of Jesus' death in our death—even the *silly* truth of his death, for silly is from the German *selig,* "blessed," and it is by the blessed foolishness of the preaching of the cross that we are saved—if we allow that death to be our only light, then we are in the light indeed. Yet one more time, in other words, Jesus exalts the "one thing necessary"—that "good part" *(agathós méros)* he commended to Martha, that quiet sitting at his nail-pierced feet—by which we find his death reigning in ours.

Next follows (Luke 11:37-54; Aland no. 194) a denunciation of the Pharisees and scribes, about which (since it will come up in its Matthean form in my final volume on the parables of judgment) I have only one thing to call to your attention here. I want you to note the recurrence of the words and themes we have been dealing with all through this chapter. He says that the Pharisees are inwardly full of violence *(harpagḗs)* and evil *(ponērías)*. A *harpagmós,* a "thing to be snatched at," is exactly what Paul, in Phil. 2:6ff., says Jesus did *not* consider his equality with God to be. Rather, he "emptied himself, taking on the form of a slave and coming in the likeness of men; and being found in outward form as a man, he humbled himself, becoming obedient to death, even a death on a cross." Enough said. And likewise enough said about *ponēría,* except to notice that right after he calls them evil, he calls them fools *(áphrones)* as well, thus underscoring the dim view he takes of the plausible, fruitless fuss by which they manage their lives.

And through the rest of his denunciation he continues, if not explicitly to exalt his death over their living, at least to bring death into the discussion. He calls them *unmarked graves.* He says they *build the graves of the prophets.* Then, stigmatizing the way their fathers *killed* the prophets and the way they *build* the prophets' tombs, he sets against all this *ponēría,* all this evil folly, the wisdom *(sophía)* of God, which he quotes as saying, "I will send them prophets and apostles, and some of them they will *kill* and persecute in order that the *blood* of all the prophets shed from the foundation of the world might be required of this generation. . . ." That's a lot of death; and true to form, the Pharisees didn't like it one bit. They set about in earnest to trap him and to do him in—never even imagining that in the death they would provide for him, he would wait to give them life. Meanwhile, he tells his disciples to "watch out for the leaven of the Pharisees, which is hypocrisy" (Luke 12:1). Precisely because their eye is *not* single—precisely because it is full of the yeasty festering of their dark, plausible designs for living—they have made themselves blind to the death that is their only source of life.

This emphasis on the darkness of human lives and on the true light that shines only out of death continues in Luke 12:2-10 (Aland nos. 196-197). Death may now be an inaccessible mystery to the world, but "nothing is covered up that will not be revealed, or hidden that will not be known. Whatever you have said in the dark [in your acceptance of the mystery of my death in yours] will be heard in the light, and what you have whispered in closed rooms [in your tomb and mine] will be proclaimed from the housetops. I tell you, my friends, do not be afraid of those who *kill* the body and after that have no more that they can do. I will show you whom to fear: fear him who, after he has *killed,* has power to cast into hell."

Once again, it is death that is safe. Hell is only for those who insist on finding their life outside of Jesus' death. Nothing, therefore, is out of control. Every sparrow counts, all the hairs of your head are numbered. "I have a whole new creation in my death and resurrection," Jesus says in effect. "So stop with all this evil, foolish pretense that you have life. Just acknowledge me before the world— confess by faith that my death is all you need—and I will acknowledge you before the angels of God. But if you won't do that, I'm afraid you're out of luck. Death and resurrection is the only game we're playing here. You can talk against *me* all you like [Luke 12:10: 'Everyone who speaks a word against the Son of man will be forgiven'], but don't knock my methods, because the Holy Spirit is groaning himself hoarse to convince you of them ['but he who blasphemes against the Holy Spirit will not be forgiven']."

Then, after two brief warnings against trying to live by getting our act together rather than by letting our passion and death happen, Jesus turns to the parable of the Rich Fool (Luke 12:16-21; Aland no. 200). Both of the warnings are about wealth. In the first (Luke 12:11-12; Aland no. 198), Jesus says the disciples are not to be anxious when they are brought before the synagogues and the rulers and the authorities. They are not to worry about what they are to answer or what they are to say. They are, in short, to be poor, and lost, and as good as dead: without the riches of a well-prepared case, without the luxury of knowing what's going to happen, and, above all, without any comforting sense that their lives are triumphantly in their own hands. And they are to be all of that because the Holy Spirit will teach them in that very hour, and not one minute before, what needs to be said. It is a warning, needless to say, that we hardly heed. Of all the desires for wealth, practically the last one we will give up is the desire for mental and spiritual richness. Yet Jesus is only urging his disciples, and us, to do what he himself did in his own trial and passion: to lay down his life and to let God raise it up in his own good time. For our comfort, even Jesus blinked at the prospect. In Gethsemane, he prayed that God would "let this cup pass" from him. But he also prayed, "nevertheless, not my will but yours be done." Poverty, not wealth—death, not life—is the only material God uses to save us.

The second warning (Luke 12:13-15; Aland no. 199) is against our less refined desire for material wealth. Someone comes to Jesus out of the crowd and says, "Teacher, tell my brother to give me my fair share of our inheritance." To which Jesus snaps back, "Hey, man, who made me a judge or divider over you people?" The man's case, no doubt, was good enough; but Jesus' ministry is not the incidental patching up of injustices. Rather it is the bearing of the final injustice—death—and the raising up from it of an entirely new and reconciled creation. Therefore he adds, "Guard yourselves against all covetousness [*pleonexía,* much-having], for a person's life does not consist in the rafts of goods that belong to him." So much for the IRAs, and the second homes, and the retirement plans that are the hope of the well-off and the envy of the poor who will never have them. Our world runs on avarice. Wealthy, poor, or in-between, we are all of us, in Jesus' eyes, nothing but unreconstructed rich people. We clutch at our lives rather than open our hands to our deaths. And as long as we do that, the real life that comes only by resurrection remains permanently out of reach.

The whole case, as I see it, is summed up in the parable of the Rich Fool. "The land of a certain rich man," Jesus tells them, "bore plentifully. And he thought to himself, 'What shall I do? I'll tear down my barns and build bigger ones, where I'll be able to store all my grain and other goods. And then I'll say to my life *[psyché]* . . .'" But stop right there. Time for a major point about scriptural wordplay.

Traditionally, the word *psyché* is translated here as "soul." But *psyché* also happens to be one of the major words in the New Testament for "life." In the immediately preceding passage, for example, Jesus says that a person's *psyché*, his life, does not consist in abundance of goods. Likewise, in the Sermon on the Mount (Matt. 6:25), he says, "Don't worry about your *psyché,* fussing about what you shall eat. . . ." The instances are too many even to begin to list them all.

Accordingly, since Jesus has, just before the Rich Fool, used *psyché* in the sense of life—and since, in this chapter, I am positively harping on his exaltation of the clean emptiness of our deaths over the messy clutter of our lives—I am taking the liberty of giving the word the odd-sounding (but, I think, tolerable) translation of "life" as it comes from the mouth of the fool. (Modern translators get around the inappropriateness of "soul" in various ways. The TEV, for instance, reads "I will say to *myself: Lucky man!*" The NEB and NIV read ". . . to *myself: Man.* . . ." Such translations get the sense of the passage pretty much right, but they fail to pick up Jesus' repetitions of the word *psyché* as he works his way through the passages at hand. Hence my preference for "life.") Back to the text.

"I will say to my life," gloats the Fool, "Life, you have ample goods laid up for many years. Take your ease, eat, drink, and be merry." Jesus, in other words, is having the Fool do what we all do in our avarice: congratulate ourselves on our lifestyle whenever possible. He sets him up as the paradigm of our whole plausible, reasonable, right-handed, wrongheaded struggle to be masters of an operation that is radically out of our control—to be captains of a ship that, all our life long, has been taking on water faster than we can bail. And then Jesus delivers the Sunday punch: "But God said to him, 'Fool! [the word is *áphrōn*, the same word he uses in denouncing the Pharisees and scribes back in Luke 11:40]. This night your life *[psyché]* is required of you; then who will own all this stuff you've spent so much time preparing?"

In a quiet last line, Jesus adds, "This is how it is with one who lays up treasure for himself and is not rich in God's sight [*eis theón*, literally, 'into God']." Jesus—upon whom the Father looks and says, "This is my beloved Son"—is the only rich man in the world; we, who spend our whole lives in the pursuit of wealth, come in the end only to the poverty of death. And we complain bitterly, unable to make head or tail of such a cruel reversal. But in Jesus—who made his grave with the wicked in their moral poverty and with the rich man in the death of all his possessing—all the pointless pursuing and all the sad incomprehension is turned to our good. He waits for us in our deaths. Quite literally, there is nothing we need to do except die.

CHAPTER NINE

Fruitfulness out of Death

The Watchful Servants and the Barren Fig Tree

The parables of the Watchful Servants (Luke 12:35-48; Aland no. 203) and of the Barren Fig Tree (Luke 13:6-9; Aland no. 207) are further illustrations of how Jesus, at this point in his ministry, uses judgment-oriented imagery but gives it a resolutely grace-governed presentation. Once again, both stories also occur later on, in Holy Week, as frankly judgmental parables (cf. Matt. 24:45-51 for the first and Matt. 21:19, as an acted parable, for the second). Here, however, Jesus' continued emphasis on death as the modus operandi of the kingdom makes them unquestionably parables of grace.

By way of a bridge from the parable of the Rich Fool with his unusable goods to the Watchful Servants and their faithful waiting, Luke gives us (in 12:22-34; Aland nos. 201-202) a catena of short, parabolic utterances. Jesus says to his disciples, "on account of this I say to you, don't worry about your life *[psychế]*, what you shall eat, etc. . . ." Jesus, as I hear him, is about to contrast the Fool's frenetic attempts at living well with the behavior of crows, lilies, and grass—creatures who quietly trust God to work in and through their mortality. He is, in other words, about to take the death that is an unqualified terror to all of us fools and display it as our only safety, our only source of the true life *(psychế)* that is "more than food." And the governing phrase—the one that specifies death as the touchstone of all these sayings—comes at the end of them (12:28). Let me put it down first, therefore, as a kind of headline: "For if God so clothes the grass in the field, which is *alive today* and *tomorrow is cast into the oven,* how much more will he clothe you, O *you of little faith?*" (italics mine).

He begins (12:24) with the ravens, who plainly are unencumbered by the kind of "life-plans" we constantly make ("they neither sow nor reap") and who, unlike us, have "neither storeroom nor barn" (*apothéke*—Jesus uses the same word in the parable of the Fool). "God nourishes them," he says; "how much different are you than birds?" Then, castigating our efforts to hold our lives together by our own devices, he says, "Which of you by worrying can add a *day to his life?*" (the phrase, as it occurs in verse 25, is *epí tēn hēlikían autoú péchyn:* it can mean either a "foot to his height" or "a day to his age"). "If you," he continues, "are not able to do even such a little thing, why do you worry about the rest?"

Then, after instancing the lilies that neither work nor make clothes for themselves, he says that "not even Solomon in all his glory was clothed like one of these." The reference to Solomon, while it can be explained simply as a convenient example of royal splendor, suggests something more profound to my ear. Back when he spoke of the Sign of Jonah (see chapter eight above)—when he said that the only sign to be given this generation would be his own death and resurrection—he added that the Queen of Sheba would "rise up *[egerthésetai]* in the judgment with the people of this generation because she came halfway around the world to hear the wisdom of Solomon, and behold, a greater than Solomon is here." Solomon's greatness lay in his life and in his lifestyle; but the greatness of the One who is greater than Solomon lies precisely in his death. Therefore when Jesus conjoins Solomon and the mortal lilies of the field, it is at least possible to take it as yet another adumbration of the theme of death and resurrection. Indeed, Jesus himself seems to have sensed the connection. He follows up the reference to Solomon with the words I quoted as a headline to this section, namely, "the grass in the field that is alive today and tomorrow is cast into the oven."

Jesus ends these comments to his disciples on the note of faith, because faith is the only thing they need once they understand that grace works entirely by raising the dead. He rebukes their care and anxiety to make a life for themselves, calling them people of "little faith." And he rebukes our faithless fussing as well.

"Everything that is not of faith is sin," says Paul in Rom. 14:23. In the last analysis, what the New Testament sets up as the opposite of sin is not virtue; it is faith. And how lucky that is for us. Precisely because virtue is not an option for the likes of us—precisely because we can no more organize our lives on good principles than we can on bad ones, and even more precisely because all the really great acts of human wickedness *(ponēría)* have always been done in the name of virtue—we are not to trust either in virtue or in our efforts to achieve it. All of that is just our life *(psyche̅)*, and for us as for the Fool, life is not something we can guarantee.

But death we can; and if we will trust him to work through it in the mystery of his death, we will find that, like the ravens and the lilies and the Queen of Sheba and the men of Nineveh, we have always been home free by the power of his resurrection. It is not a matter of our knowing it or feeling it—or of our working up plausible, right-handed devices for laying hold of it. "No man," Luther said, "can know or feel he is saved; he can only believe it." Therefore it is by faith alone that we can lay hold of our true life out of death— faith in him who is the resurrection and the life. All we have to do is trust Jesus and die. Everything else has already been done. The ravens and the lilies bear mute testimony to that trust; our joy waits until we give voice to what they already express.

Our death, therefore, is the one "purse that will never wear out," the true "treasure in heaven that will never decrease." We are rich only in our mortality; everything else may safely be sold (Luke 12:33). For our death is the only thing the world cannot take away from us. The goods on which our heart now reposes can be removed from us, or we from them, in a night: the thief, the moth, and the changes and chances of this mortal life are always and everywhere one giant step ahead of us. But if we repose our hearts upon the faith that he works in our death, we cannot lose. The astonishing graciousness of grace is that it takes the one thing you and I will never lack—the one thing, furthermore, that no one will ever want to beg, borrow, or steal from us—and makes it the only thing any of us will ever need. It was, I think, precisely because the martyrs bore witness to this saving supremacy of death that they were the first saints commemorated by the church. Indeed, the days of their deaths were commonly referred to as their *natales,* their birthdays. It was one of the church's happier insights. For as in our first birth into this world we did nothing and triumphed gloriously, so in the second birth of our death we need do even less to triumph more. By Jesus' death in ours, and by our death in his, we have laughingly, uproariously, outrageously beaten the system. It is a piece of wildly Good News: what a shame we don't let the world of losers hear it more often.

Indeed, it is this very note of stewardship of the Gospel of grace—of readiness to comply with and to proclaim its absurdly minimal demands—that is evident in the way Jesus begins the immediately following parable of the Watchful Servants (Luke 12:35-48; Aland no. 203). "Let your loins be girded about and your lamps burning," he says to the disciples. "You have," he tells them in effect, "an incredibly cheerful piece of intelligence to impart to the desperate winners out there who are panicked at the thought of their inevitable losing. I don't want you bumbling around in their darkness with the pants of your trust down around your ankles for lack of the girding of faith in my death." But he opens the parable itself with an even more pregnant bit of imagery: "And you yourselves must be like men who are waiting for their lord [*kýrion*] to come back from a wedding [*ek tōn gámōn*]. . . ."

Time for another halt. One of my convictions about interpreting Jesus' parables is that it is always a mistake to say too quickly what we think is their "main point." Had he wanted to give us glittering generalities, he could no doubt have unburdened himself of them in plain Aramaic and avoided the bother of having to make up artful stories. But in fact he did tell stories; and since he was no slouch at crafting them, we should spend more time than we do on their details—especially when the detail is as rich a one as the wedding Jesus sketches in here.

Let me illustrate by introducing two other New Testament uses of the imagery of the wedding: the Marriage at Cana where Jesus performed his first sign *(sēmeíon)*, turning water into wine (John 2:1-11); and the Marriage of the Lamb to his Bride, the New Jerusalem, at the very end of the Bible (Rev. 19:7-9 and 21:1–22:17, passim). These two passages—in which a wedding reception is used to delineate major events in the history of salvation—make me suspicious of interpretations that dismiss the wedding party in the parable of the Watchful Servants as nothing more than a minor detail. Had Jesus wanted simply to get the lord of the servants home unpredictably late, he could have arranged for him to be tied up in traffic on the freeway, or stuck in an all-night diner with a boring friend. But Jesus says it was precisely a wedding that delayed the lord's coming. And he uses that device, I think, because of a bizarre connection in his mind—or at least in the mind of the Spirit who presides over the Scriptures—between weddings and death.

Consider the Cana story first. When Jesus' mother tells him that the party they are both attending has just run out of wine, he gives her a cryptic reply: "What's that to me and you, woman? *My hour [hē hōra mou]* has not yet come." In the literary shorthand of John's Gospel, *hōra* (hour, time) is one of the words used to refer to the climactic events of Jesus' ministry, namely, his passion, death, and resurrection. Furthermore, in the peculiarly transposed time-sequence of John, the Wedding at Cana is followed immediately by the cleansing of the temple—which, in all the other Gospels, occurs in Holy Week. Somebody therefore (either Jesus, John, the Spirit, or all three) saw a connection between the two events. So much so, that in the Johannine version of the casting out of the money-changers, Jesus actually makes a parabolic reference to his coming death. When asked what sign he is showing by thus cleansing the temple, he replies, "Destroy this temple and in three days I will raise it up." The reference, of course, is to his own body's death and resurrection—in other words, to nothing less than the Sign of Jonah all over again.

As for the second passage, the Marriage of the Lamb to his Bride in the Book of Revelation is equally fraught with death. Notice the details. The Lamb is none other than the *Lamb Slain:* the crucified, risen Redeemer. In addition, the saints—the citizens of the New Jerusalem that comes down from heaven as a bride prepared for her husband—have "washed their robes and made them white in the blood of the Lamb" (Rev. 7:14).

And as if those two passages were not enough importing of death into the imagery of marriage, consider Jesus' parable of the King's Son's Wedding (Matt. 22:1-14), in which death is liberally poured over all the proceedings: the first-invited guests *kill* the messengers bringing the King's invitation; the King himself, in response, *destroys* those *murderers* and *burns up* their city.

You may, of course, have your doubts as to whether Jesus had all that in mind when he began the parable of the Watchful Servants. But since you can't prove he didn't any more than I can prove he did, your argument, so dear to critical minds, ends in a draw. In any case, I am not so much concerned to guess what Jesus may have had in mind as I am to comment on what the church, in the Scriptures, has preserved of what he actually said. But since I believe the Holy Spirit presided effectively over the formation of Scripture, I do feel at least a bit free to try guessing what the *Spirit* may have had in mind when he fingered in all this imagery of the wedding.

Let your mind *play* with the scriptural parallels therefore. The lord of the servants—who is, after all, the Christ-figure in this parable—comes to them from a nuptial feast. Correspondingly, the Lord Jesus—whom the Book of Revelation (22:20) asks to "come"—comes to the consummation of history from his own nuptials as the Lamb Slain. The servants, to take another parallel, are described as waiting expectantly to open to the lord when he comes and knocks; we, their counterparts, are to be ready to welcome the Lamb Slain when he "stands at the door and knocks" (Rev. 3:20). Finally, when the lord comes and finds his servants watching, they are blessed because "he will gird himself with a servant's towel and make them sit down *and he will come and serve them.*" Their great good luck is that he will come home in a hilarious mood. He will not come with sober assessments of past performances or with grim orders for future exertions; rather he will come with a song in his tipsy heart, a chilled bottle of Dom Perignon in each tail of his coat, and a breakfast to end all breakfasts in his hands: bacon, sausage, grits, homefries, and eggs sunny-side up. We too, then, are blessed in the risen Jesus, for he comes to us from his nuptials in death, and asks only that we wait in faith for him. He will knock at the door of our own death, and he will come in and throw us a party (Rev. 3:20; 19:7-9).

The imagery of the coming of the Lord in this parable, therefore, is party imagery: Jesus comes to us from a party, and he brings the party with him. Moreover, he has made it clear that he will keep the party going both now and forever: now, in the mystery of the Lord's Supper by which we celebratively "show forth the Lord's death till he comes" (1 Cor. 11:26); and forever, at the "Supper of the Lamb" (Rev. 19:9) where we will "sit together with him in heavenly places" (Eph. 2:6) as his "Bride" (Revelation, passim).

Whether that sort of commentary is exegesis, eisegesis, both, or neither, I don't know and don't care. My only reason for offering it is that it has the virtue of letting Scripture comment on Scripture. For it is only when that happens that you begin to get a hint of the richness of biblical imagery. In fact, I am disposed to press the wedding image even harder and say that the whole of Scripture, from Genesis to Revelation, is one long development of the theme of boy meets girl, boy loses girl, boy gets girl.

Watch. The Word—who in response to the Father's good pleasure woos creation into being out of nothing—meets the world in the first and second chapters of Genesis and falls head over divine heels in love with it. But in Genesis 3, the world turns its back on the Word and wanders lost in death. Then, in most of the rest of Scripture, the Word unceasingly seeks in death for the beloved he lost: he seeks for her in the passion and defeat of Israel in the Old Testament and in the death of the incarnate Lord in the New. Finally, in the Book of Revelation, by his winsome power as the Lamb Slain, the Word courts the world once and for all: at the end of the story, Boy gets girl, makes her his bride, and takes her home to his Father's house forever.

It is a consummation eminently worth waiting for; and it is the joyful safeness of that waiting that is the principal burden of the parable of the Watchful Servants. For as Jesus tells the story, even if the lord of the servants comes at midnight or later, they are blessed because his will is only to come in and sup with them. And as the parable applies to us, no one who waits for Jesus in faith can ever wait too long for him to come or ever be in any danger of missing the bus on which he comes. For he comes, not on the uncertain bus of our lives but on the absolutely certain bus of our death. He comes, to ring a change on the phrase, in the utterly dependable act of our *missing the bus* altogether. All we need to watch out for is that we take no other buses, however plausible—that we be content to sit still at the bus stop of his death in ours. And that, if you will, is what the word "ready" means at the end of this parable (Luke 12:40). "The Son of man," Jesus says, "comes at a time you don't think" (*hē hōrą ou dokeíte,* in an hour that seems like nothing to you). To be "ready" for that, therefore, all you have to do is wait in faith for *nothing*—that is, for death. And the only way of being unready is to cut short that waiting by unfaith—to dash off on material or spiritual excursions we think will give us life. But our life does not consist in the abundance of things we possess (Luke 12:15). Rather our life is hid with Christ in God (Col. 3:3) in the mystery of Jesus' death and resurrection. He who loses his life for Jesus' sake, therefore, will find it (Matt. 10:39).

Hearing all this, Peter says to Jesus, "Lord, are you telling this parable to us, or to everybody?" Jesus answers him with yet another parable: "Who then is the faithful *[pistós]* and wise *[phrónimos]* steward whom the lord will set over his household to give them their share of food at the proper time? Blessed is that servant, if the lord, when he comes, finds him so doing. Truly I tell you, that he will put him in charge of all his property."

While Jesus' reply can no doubt be given a reading that extends it to the "everybody" Peter asked about, it seems to me the most natural interpretation is to take it as referring to the disciples and, by extension, to their successors, the clergy: that is, to all the stewards of the Gospel in their several generations.

In the light of this text, then, preachers of the Word labor under three distinct requirements. First, they are to be faithful *(pistoí)*. They are called to believe, and they are called only to believe. They are not called to know, or to be clever, or to be proficient, or to be energetic, or to be talented, or to be well-adjusted. Their vocation is simply to be faithful waiters on the mystery of Jesus' coming in death and resurrection. What the world needs to hear from them is not any of their ideas, bright or dim: none of those can save a single soul. Rather, it needs to hear—and above all to see—their own commitment to the ministry of waiting for, and waiting on, the only Lord who has the keys of death (Rev. 1:18).

Second, the clergy are to be wise *(phrónimoi)*. They are not to be fools, rich or poor, who think that salvation can come to anyone as a result of living. The world is already drowning in its efforts at life; it does not need lifeguards who swim to it carrying the barbells of their own moral and spiritual efforts. Preachers are to come honestly empty-handed to the world, because anyone who comes bearing more than the folly of the *kérygma*—of the preaching of the word of the cross (1 Cor. 1:21, 18)—has missed completely the foolishness *(mōrón)* of God that is wiser *(sophóteron)* than men. The wise *(phrónimos)* steward, therefore, is the one who knows that God has stood all known values on their heads—that, as Paul says in 1 Cor. 1:26ff., he has not chosen the wise, or the mighty, or the socially adept, but rather that he has chosen what the world considers nonsense *(ta mōrá)* in order to shame the wise *(sophoús)*, and what the world considers weak *(ta asthené)* in order to shame the strong. The clergy are worth their salt only if they understand that God deals out salvation solely through the klutzes *(ta agené)* and the nobodies *(ta exouthenéména)* of the world—through, in short, the last, the least, the lost, the little, and the dead. If they think God is waiting for them to provide them with classier help, they should do everybody a favor and get out of the preaching business. Let them do less foolish work. Let them sell junk bonds.

But it is the third of these clerical requirements that strikes me as the most telling: preachers are stewards whom the Lord has "set over his household servants to provide them with food at the proper time." After all the years the church has suffered under forceful preachers and winning orators, under compelling pulpiteers and clerical bigmouths with egos to match, how nice to hear that Jesus expects preachers in their congregations to be nothing more than faithful household cooks. Not gourmet chefs, not banquet managers, not caterers to thousands, just Gospel pot-rattlers who can turn out a decent, nourishing meal once a week. And not even a whole meal, perhaps; only the right food at the proper time. On most Sundays, maybe all it has to be is meat, pasta, and a vegetable. Not every sermon needs to be prefaced by a cocktail hour full of the homiletical equivalent of Vienna sausages and bacon-wrapped water chestnuts; nor need nourishing preaching always be dramatically concluded with a dessert of flambéed sentiment and souffléed prose. The preacher has only to deliver food, not flash; Gospel, not uplift. And the preacher's congregational family doesn't even have to like it. If it's good food at the right time, they can bellyache all they want: as long as they get enough death and resurrection, some day they may even realize they've been well fed.

So much for the faithful preacher. Jesus, however, does not end his answer to Peter there. "But if," he continues, "that servant says in his heart, 'My lord is certainly taking his own sweet time about coming,' and if he begins to smack his fellow waiters and waitresses around, and to eat and drink and get drunk. . . ." If, that is, the preacher gets tired of the foolishness of the Gospel and begins to amuse himself with his own versions of intelligible fun and games—whether by exploiting his fellow servants bodies, or by intellectually devouring their souls like cheese puffs—then the Lord of that preacher "will come on a day he does not expect and at a time [*hóra* again] he does not know, and he will cut him up in little pieces and appoint his portion [*méros*] with the unfaithful [*apístōn*]."

Only one thing is necessary, therefore, and that is the "good part" *(agathós méros)* that Mary chose and Martha despised. All that preachers need to do is sit at the feet of Jesus on the cross and preach out of their fidelity to that sitting. But if they will not do that, the only thing left for them is the "part of the unfaithful": the slow or sudden falling to pieces of their lives by virtue of their very efforts to live them. Because they will not choose the emptiness of being faithful *(pistós)*, the only thing left for them is to live by what they think they know. But because they are not wise—not *phrónimoi*, not aware that the only thing that counts any more is the foolishness of the cross—then all the two-bit pomposities they substitute for the saving simplicity will simply bore them and everyone else to tears. They will, like Ahimaaz (2 Sam. 18:19ff.), be nothing but breathless messengers who never figured out what the message was supposed to be.

Jesus therefore wraps up the parable of the Watchful Servants with a warning that needs almost no comment: "That servant who knew the will of his lord but did not ready himself *[mē hetoimásas]*, or act *[poiēsas]* according to that will, will be skinned royally *[darēsetai pollás]*. But he who did not know, even if he did things worthy of a real beating *[plēgōn]*, will be skinned only lightly *[darēsetai olígas]*. For from the one to whom much has been given much will be required; and from the one to whom people have committed much they will demand the more." Jesus came to raise the dead; he saves by no other means. If the clergy cannot be faithful to the muchness of that little, they really would be better off selling junk bonds.

Between the parable of the Watchful Servants and the parable of the Barren Fig Tree, Luke interposes some sayings of Jesus that continue his emphasis on death rather than living as the means of salvation. For brevity's sake—and since the point has already been belabored—let me give you only some notes on the passages in question (Luke 12:49–13:5; Aland nos. 204-207).

Luke 12:49-59 (Jesus as Cause of Division): "I came to cast fire on the earth; and what do I care if it's already kindled! I have a baptism to be baptized with and how distressed I am until it is consummated *[telesthē]*! Do you think I came to give peace on earth? No, I tell you, rather division." And Jesus continues in the same vein, listing samples of the way his ministry will disrupt all our efforts at normal, proper living: households divided two against three, father against son, daughter against mother, and so on.

This is quite plainly death-talk. *Item: Baptism.* John baptizes only with water; Jesus will baptize with the Holy Spirit and with fire (Matt. 3:11). *Item: Jesus refers to his death as his baptism.* James and John (Mark 10:35ff.) want to sit on his right and his left in glory; Jesus says they don't know what they're asking for. "Are you able," he asks, "to drink the cup I drink [an anticipation of 'let this cup pass from me' in Gethsemane: e.g., Matt. 26:39], or to be baptized with the baptism with which I am baptized?" *Item: "Until it is consummated" [telesthē̂].* The root of the Greek word reappears dramatically at the very point of Jesus' death on the cross: "*Tetélestai,*" he says (John 19:30), "it is finished, *consummatum est.*" *Item: "Not peace but division."* God's insistence on death-resurrection as the method of salvation will play hob with all sensible approaches to life. People will fight rather than switch from the prudent wisdom of ordinary living to the scandal and the foolishness of a crucified Messiah (1 Cor. 1:21-25).

Luke 12:54-56 (Interpreting the Times): Item: Jesus tells the crowds, "when you see a cloud rising in the west, you say, 'A rainstorm is coming,' and that's what happens; and when the south wind is blowing you say, 'It's going to be a scorcher,' and it is." He compliments them, in other words, on their ability to read—and to accept and adjust to—the signs of the natural disruptions of their designs for ordinary living. They will cancel a picnic, for example: they will accept the death that the rainstorm imposes on their plans for the day and they will rise out of it into something totally new, like an afternoon with a good mystery. But then he calls them hypocrites: "How come," he asks them, "you can be so discerning about these natural signs of disruption in earth and sky, but you can't discern this present time?" He is going to Jerusalem and his death. And he is going there in order to make death and disruption safe—to make it the very means of grace and salvation. But when he says in plain words that he's going, nobody really hears him (Jesus has already predicted his death and resurrection twice, e.g., Luke 9:22 and 9:43-45), and when he talks to them in parables about it, all their native intelligence evaporates. *Item: "This present time" (ton kairón toúton).* The word *kairós* means "time" in the sense of "due season" or "high time," as opposed to "clock time" (which in Greek is *chrónos*). *Kairós* here, therefore, echoes the significance of the word *hóra*, "hour," as used in the Watchful Servants, and of the words *hē hóra mou*, "my hour," "the time of my death," as used throughout the Gospel of John.

Luke 12:57-59 (Settling with One's Accuser): Jesus holds up litigiousness as an example of the way people's lives are in fact made worse by their efforts to get the due rewards of their living. He says they would be better off dropping their suit on the way to court—advice which, to determined plaintiffs, is tantamount to telling them to drop dead. The whole passage, in fact, anticipates another saying from the passion narrative, namely, Jesus' words in Gethsemane: "those who take the sword will perish by the sword" (Matt. 26:52).

Luke 13:1-5 (Jesus on Current Horror Stories): Some enthusiasts of the kind of journalism featured at supermarket checkout counters ("Mom Ices Baby in Freezer!" "Scoutmaster Goes Beserk with Bazooka!") regale Jesus with an atrocity story. Pilate, they tell him, killed some Galileans and poured their blood on their own altars. "So?" Jesus replies. "You think that because these Galileans suffered such a horrible death, they were some kind of super-sinners? No way! But unless you repent, you will all likewise perish." Then he adds an item of his own from the tabloids ("Siloam Tower Collapses; Kills Eighteen!"). His point? Well, I hardly think he was saying that if they could manage to repent of their sins, they wouldn't die: the way the Gospel works out, even being sinless can't guarantee that. In fact, it guarantees just the opposite: a still more horrible death on the cross. Maybe what he was telling them to repent of was actually their rejection of death—a rejection they compensated for by whistling in the dark and telling horror stories. Maybe they were supposed to stop pretending death was something God sent only to bad guys and realize it was his chosen way of saving even people with lives as carefully lived as theirs. "You're *all* going to die," Jesus tells them in effect. "But since I'm going to die for you and with you, maybe you should stop trying to keep death at arm's length. You have nothing to lose but your horror."

In any case, it is just this acceptance of death that Jesus continues to press in the next parable, the story of the Barren Fig Tree (Luke 13:6-9; Aland no. 207). The episode of the fig tree appears in all three synoptic Gospels. Only in Luke, however, is it presented as a story told by Jesus on the way to Jerusalem; in Matthew and Mark, it appears in Holy Week as an *acted parable*—with Jesus himself actually cursing the fig tree and the fig tree withering away.

According to my division of the parables, therefore, the actual cursing of the fig tree should turn out to be a parable of judgment; and the story version, by its placement well before the events of Holy Week, should turn out to be a parable of grace. Not that the two categories are mutually exclusive: the parable of the Barren Fig Tree, by its very nature, is about judgment, crisis, the time of decision. But it is also about the unique way in which the judgment is, for now at least, suspended in favor of grace. In this, the Barren Fig Tree is a companion piece to Jesus' earlier parable of the Wheat and the Weeds. In both stories, a perfectly correct *judgment* on a bad situation gives way to a *letting be,* to a *suffering* of the badness—to an *áphesis,* that is, that both permits and forgives the evil (the Greek *aphiénai* variously means to let, allow, permit, suffer, pardon, forgive).

Consider the story, then. A certain man has a fig tree planted in his vineyard and he comes to it looking for figs and finds none. So he says to his vinedresser, "Three years I've been trying to get figs from this tree and it hasn't produced even one. Cut it down. Why should it use up ground?" But the vinedresser says to him, "Let it be, Lord *[kýrie áphes autén],* for one year more, till I dig around it and put on manure. If it bears fruit next year, so much the better; if not, then you'll cut it down."

Look first at the details of the parable. It may not be wise to put too much weight on the fact that the fig tree is planted in a vineyard: people probably planted both in the same space and Scripture certainly seems to consider "vines and fig trees" companion plantings. But there is at least a suggestion here that the lord in the parable is principally a grape grower (he has, apparently, a full-time vinedresser) and that he has planted the fig tree more out of personal delight than out of entrepreneurial practicality. Plainly, then, since the fig tree stands for the human side of the parabolic picture (for the Jerusalem Jews, or for Judaism in general, or for the whole human race: take your pick), Jesus seems to be saying that the world is more God's hobby than his business, that it exists more for pleasure than for profit. God's attitude toward the world, therefore, involves *favor* from the start; grace is not something he drags in later on just to patch up messes. Unnecessary, spontaneous delight is the very root of his relationship with the world.

There is a complication, however, in the next set of details. Not, of course, in the part about seeking figs and finding none: that simply stands for God's disappointment with whatever it is you decide to let the fig tree represent. But when Jesus introduces the vinedresser into the parable—and then proceeds to make *him* the source of the decision to exercise grace instead of judgment—he takes a new tack. It would have been just as easy for Jesus to make the lord of the vineyard himself the originator of the gracious beneficence (as he did, for example, in the parable of the Laborers in the Vineyard, Matt. 20:1-16). At this point, though, Jesus is not content to leave things that simple. As he does in a few other places, he casts two characters in the divine role: one to represent the Father (the divine beneficence in its judgmental aspect) and the other to represent the Son (the divine beneficence as grace). Needless to say, it is the second of these characters that turns out, somewhat bizarrely, to be the Christ-figure in the parable (see the Unjust Steward, chapter fourteen below, for the most bizarre instance of all).

In any case, it is the vinedresser who is the Christ-figure here. It is precisely because he, underling though he is, invites the owner of the vineyard into forbearance and forgiveness that the barren fig tree continues to live by grace. *"Áphes,"* he says to his lord: *"Let it be."* And it is just that word that makes him one of the clearest Christ-figures in all the parables. For on the cross, in the very teeth of death, Jesus himself says, *"Áphes,* forgive."

Note, too, the vinedresser's last line: he says to his lord, "If it doesn't bear fruit next year, then *you* will cut it down." I'm not sure what that says about God the Father, but I'm certain it says that God the Son—who is the only one who offers the reconciled creation to the Father, and to whom the Father has in fact committed all judgment (John 5:22)—will never go back on the *áphesis* he has pronounced over the world. "I did not come to judge the world," Jesus said, "but to save the world" (John 12:47).

The world lives, as the fig tree lives, under the rubric of forgiveness. The world, of course, thinks otherwise. In its blind wisdom, it thinks it lives by merit and reward. It likes to imagine that salvation is essentially a pat on the back from a God who either thinks we are good eggs or, if he knows how rotten we actually are, considers our repentance sufficient to make up for our unsuitability. But by the foolishness of God, that is not the way it works. By the folly of the cross, Jesus becomes sin for us, and he goes outside the camp for us, and he is relegated to the dump for us, and he becomes garbage and compost, offal and manure for us. And then he comes to us. The Vinedresser who on the cross said *"áphes"* to his Lord and Father comes to us with his own body dug deep by nails and spears, and his own being made dung by his death, and he sends our roots resurrection. He does not come to see if we are good: he comes to disturb the caked conventions by which we pretend to be good. He does not come to see if we are sorry: he knows our repentance isn't worth the hot air we put into it. He does not come to count *anything*. Unlike the lord in the parable, he cares not even a fig for any part of our record, good or bad. He comes only to forgive. For free. For nothing. On no basis, because like the fig tree, we are too far gone to have a basis. On no conditions, because like the dung of death he digs into our roots, he is too dead to insist on prerogatives. We are saved gratis, by grace. We do nothing and we deserve nothing; it is all, absolutely and without qualification, one huge, hilarious gift.

And all because there is indeed a Vinedresser. I can love Jesus. As I said, I don't know about his Father. The only thing I can say about God the Father is that he's lucky to have such a lovable Son. Sometimes I think that if I had to go by his track record instead of just taking Jesus' word for his good character, I wouldn't give him the time of day. And I don't know about the Holy Spirit either. So much hot air has been let off in his name that if Jesus hadn't said he was sending him, I'd write him off too. But Jesus I can love. He does everything, I do nothing; I just trust him. It is a nifty arrangement, and for a deadbeat like me, it is the only one that can possibly work. As long as I am in him, I bear fruit. As long as his death feeds my roots, I will never be cut down.

> Jesus, Jesus, Jesus:
> Jesus, Jesus, Jesus;
> Jesus, Jesus, Jesus, Jesus,
> I love you, I love you, I love you.

CHAPTER TEN

Interlude on an Objection

Why Not Life Rather Than Death?

If I assess your mood correctly, it is time to take a break. You have listened for a long time now to what must seem like a monomaniacal insistence on death, and you have just about had it with all this talk about free grace. "What ever happened," you want to object, "to the positive idea of Christian *living*? If all we have to do to be saved is drop dead, why bother even trying to live—especially, why bother to be good, loving, or moral? Why not just go out and sin all we like? What role have you left for religion in the world, if everybody is going to get home free for nothing?"

Let me interrupt your train of thought right there, because you are beginning to drift away from the point of your most telling objection, namely, my failure to deal with the legitimate subject of living. I shall get to that in a moment. First, though, I want to lay to rest the last two ghosts you just let loose.

What role have I left for religion? None. And I have left none because the Gospel of our Lord and Savior Jesus Christ leaves none. Christianity is not a religion; it is the announcement of the end of religion. Religion consists of all the things (believing, behaving, worshiping, sacrificing) the human race has ever thought it had to do to get right with God. About those things, Christianity has only two comments to make. The first is that none of them ever had the least chance of doing the trick: the blood of bulls and goats can never take away sins (see the Epistle to the Hebrews) and no effort of ours to keep the law of God can ever succeed (see the Epistle to the Romans). The second is that everything religion tried (and failed) to do has been perfectly done, once and for all, by Jesus in his death and resurrection. For Christians, therefore, the entire religion shop has been closed, boarded up, and forgotten. The church is not in the religion business. It never has been and it never will be, in spite of all the ecclesiastical turkeys through two thousand years who have acted as if religion was their stock in trade. The church, instead, is in the Gospel-proclaiming business. It is not here to bring the world the bad news that God will think kindly about us only after we have gone through certain creedal, liturgical, and ethical wickets; it is here to bring the world the Good News that "while we were yet sinners, Christ died for the ungodly." It is here, in short, for no religious purpose at all, only to announce the Gospel of free grace.

Your other ghost can be laid to rest just as quickly. The reason for not going out and sinning all you like is the same as the reason for not going out and putting your nose in a slicing machine: it's dumb, stupid, and no fun. Some individual *sins* may have pleasure still attached to them because of the residual goodness of the realities they are abusing: adultery can indeed be pleasant, and tying one on can amuse. But betrayal, jealousy, love grown cold, and the gray dawn of the morning after are nobody's idea of a good time.

On the other hand, there's no use belaboring that point, because it never stopped anybody. And neither did religion. The notion that people won't sin as long as you keep them well supplied with guilt and holy terror is a bit overblown. Giving the human race religious reasons for not sinning is about as useful as reading lectures to an elephant in rut. We have always, in the pinches, done what we damn pleased, and God has let us do it. His answer to sin is not to scream "Stop that!" but to shut up once and for all on the subject in Jesus' death.

Furthermore, the usual objection to God's silence, namely, that people will take such graciousness on his part as *permission* to sin, is equally nonsensical. For one thing, he made us free, so we already have his permission—not his advice, mind you, nor his consent, nor his enthusiasm—but definitely his promise not to treat us like puppets. For another, few of us, at the point of sinning, actually run around trying to get someone to sign a permission slip for us; we just go ahead full steam on our own. And for the final thing, the whole idea of people actually being *encouraged* to seduce maidens, or water stock, or poison wells by the agony and death of Jesus on the cross is simply ludicrous. We ourselves, thank you very much, are all the encouragement we need for dastardly deeds.

I am left, therefore, with the unhappy suspicion that people who are afraid the preaching of grace will encourage sin are in fact people who resent the righteousness they have forced themselves into. Having led "good" lives—and worse yet, having denied themselves the pleasures of sin—they seethe inwardly at any suggestion that God may not be as hard on drug pushers and child molesters as they always thought he would be on themselves.

But enough of religion and morality, those two doughty substitutes for living. What about your really considerable objection? What about the charge that in exalting death as the means of grace, I have utterly neglected the subject of the Christian life? I plead guilty. I have neglected it. But only because I think that Jesus, at this point in his career, is neglecting it too. Still, I shall meet you halfway: I shall give you a few assurances that I still consider living a genuine possibility for faithful Christians; and then I shall give you an example of the kind of living I have in mind when I say we are to be "dead" even before our final death.

Life is good. God invented it, and when it is lived according to his designs, it can be terrific. And the designs of God—the laws, physical and moral, by which life is meant to be governed—are nothing less than his specifications for the beauties of his several creatures. The law, therefore—moral law in particular, but physical law as well—is precisely our beauty; and insofar as we succeed in living lawfully, we enjoy our own gorgeousness just as God enjoys it. Moreover, even in our present fallen world, the goodness of good living (physical or moral) is still available to us. Christians therefore, in gratitude to God, continue to live and to pursue goodness of all sorts: the pleasures of sports, the delights of the mind, the joys of mutual affection, the consolations of nature, the satisfactions of virtuous and kindly acts—no lawful action, high or low, great or small, is ever an inconsiderable thing to a Christian.

However. But. Still. Nevertheless. In spite of all that. The Gospel truth is that neither we nor the world can be saved by efforts at living well. If the human race could have straightened up its act by the simple pursuit of goodness, it would have done so long ago. We are not stupid; and Lord knows, from Confucius to Socrates to Moses to Joyce Brothers, we've had plenty of advice. But we haven't followed it. The world has taken a five-thousand-year bath in wisdom and is just as grimy as ever. And our own lives now, for all our efforts to clean them up, just get grimier and grimier. We think pure thoughts and eat wheat germ bread, but we will die as our fathers did, not noticeably better.

Once again, the world cannot be saved by living. And there are two devastatingly simple reasons why. The first is, we don't live well enough to do the job. Our goodness is flawed goodness. I love my children and you love yours, but we have, both of us, messed them up royally. I am a nice person and so are you, except for when my will is crossed or your convenience is not consulted—and then we are both so fearful that we get mean in order to seem tough. And so on. The point is that if we are going to wait for good living to save the world, we are going to wait a long time. We can see goodness and we can love it. We can even love it enough to get a fair amount of it going for us on nice days. But we simply cannot crank it up to the level needed to eliminate badness altogether.

The second reason is more profound. The world's deepest problem is not badness as opposed to goodness; it is *sin,* the incurable human tendency to put self first, to trust number one and no one else. And that means that there is nothing—no right deed, however good, noble, lawful, thrifty, brave, clean, or reverent—that cannot be done for the wrong reason, that cannot be tainted and totally corrupted by sin. As I observed earlier, the greatest evils are, with alarming regularity, done in the name of goodness. When we finally fry this planet in a nuclear holocaust, it will not have been done by a bunch of naughty little boys and girls; it will have been done by grave, respectable types who loved their high ideals too much to lay them down for the mere preservation of life on earth. And lesser evils follow the same rule. When I crippled my children emotionally (or when my parents crippled me) it was not done out of meanness or spite, it was done out of love: genuine, deeply felt, endlessly pondered human love—flawed, alas, by a self-regard so profound that none of us ever noticed it.

Life, therefore, for all its goodness—the act of living, for all its lawfulness and even occasional success—cannot save. I am sorry to disappoint you, but we are back at death—faith in Jesus' death—as the only reliable guide, the only effective opposite to *sin,* which otherwise can play havoc with goodness and badness alike. But let me take the edge off that by giving you an illustration of what death as a way of living might be like. The temptation, of course, is to imagine it as a doing of nothing at all, a profound quietism, a deadly, boring wait for death itself finally to turn up and end the nag. To help you get around that view, I want you to hold out your right hand, palm up, and imagine that someone is placing, one after another, all sorts of good gifts in it. Make the good things whatever you like—M & Ms, weekends in Acapulco, winning the lottery, falling in love, having perfect children, being wise, talented, good-looking, and humble besides—anything. But now consider. There are two ways your hand can respond to those goods. It can respond to them as a live hand and try to clutch, to hold onto the single good that is in it at any given moment—thus closing itself to all other possible goods; or it can respond as a dead hand—in which case it will simply lie there perpetually open to all the goods in the comings and the goings of their dance.

When I talk about being dead, accordingly, I have in mind not the absence of interest in the dance of living, but the absence of clutching at our partners in the dance—not *not-dancing,* if you will, but *not-trying-to-stop-the-dance.* In a way, that is nothing more than gurus and spiritual advisers the world over have been saying for millennia. But it is also, I think, quite specifically the way the Gospel invites us to live. Jesus, obviously, was not without an interest in life: his reputation as a glutton and winebibber was not gained by sitting at home eating tofu and drinking herb tea. But equally obviously, Jesus did not count his life—either human or divine—a thing to be grasped at. He was open at all times to what God put into his hand and he remained faithful in that openness until death—at which point God, by the power of the resurrection, put the whole world in his hand.

Think "dead hand," then: it is the only way, here or hereafter, that life can safely be enjoyed.

CHAPTER ELEVEN

Back to Death, Lastness, and Lostness

The Mustard Seed, the Yeast, and the Narrow Door

The next group of parables runs from Luke 13:10 to 13:30 (Aland nos. 208-211) and includes the Mustard Seed, the Yeast, and the Narrow Door. In these, Jesus not only continues his emphasis on death but also returns with considerable force to the themes of lastness and lostness as touchstones of the operation of grace.

The section begins with Jesus' healing of a crippled woman (Luke 13:10-17; Aland no. 208). This story, which is parabolic only to the extent that it contains Jesus' usual sprinkling of colorful comparisons, nonetheless has a bearing on my interpretation of the parables. The healing, we are told, took place in a synagogue on the sabbath—to the annoyance of the authorities of the congregation. Jesus, of course, violated the sabbath in various ways right from the start of his ministry; but it is worth asking whether his breaking of it now sheds a light different from that of earlier occasions.

I think it does. In those first violations of the injunction to do no work on the sabbath, Jesus was at pains to vindicate his own authority. Justifying his "hand-milling" of grain on the sabbath, for example, he said, "the Son of man is lord even of the sabbath" (Mark 2:28). But in the developed Christian imagery of the sabbath, a new emphasis, above and beyond the original one of rest, comes to the fore. It is an emphasis on death; and I want to enter it into the record here as Jesus comes closer and closer to the death he is courting on this final journey to Jerusalem. Let me give you, therefore, a few notes about the sabbath—remembering, if you will, that I am using the word, even in Christian contexts, to refer to Saturday. (Sunday, for Christians, is not the sabbath; it is the First Day of the Week, the

Lord's Day, *Dies Dominica,* celebrated in honor of the resurrection. In the Romance languages, the name for Saturday comes from the Hebrew—e.g., the Italian *Sabbato;* the name for Sunday comes from the Latin for Lord's Day—e.g., the French *Dimanche*).

Item. In the old covenant, the sabbath is a day of rest in honor of God's work of creation; in the new covenant, the sabbath becomes a day of death—the day Jesus' body lay in the tomb, the day *Christ lag in Totesbanden.*

Item: Christian liturgical terminology. Jesus dies on *Good Friday,* which, in addition to being the eve of the sabbath, is also the preparation of the Passover. And he rises on *Easter Sunday,* which is the first day of the working week. But the day in between is called, variously, *Easter Even, Holy Saturday,* or *The Holy Sabbath, Sabbato Sancto.*

Item: Easter Even. The great service on this day is the *Easter Vigil,* whose theme is the renewal of creation by the resurrection of Jesus from the dead (the entire first creation story, Gen. 1:1–2:3, is the first of many lessons recapitulating the history of salvation from the old covenant to the new). In other words, as the church on Holy Saturday sits quietly in the tomb with the dead Christ, it also sits joyfully, believing that, in Jesus, death has been made twice as creative as the act of creation ever was. The death of Jesus, therefore, is not just something that lasted through a single sabbath day in the spring of A.D. 29. Precisely because he who was dead that day was the Incarnate Lord, the Second Person of the triune God, his death is an eternal as well as a temporal fact. Jesus is not only risen forever; he is also dead forever. The heavenly sabbaths we look forward to celebrating will be a perpetual renewal of creation, proceeding by a perpetual resurrection out of a perpetual death.

> *O quanta qualia sunt illa sabbata,*
> *quae semper celebrat superna curia,*
> *quae fessis requies, quae merces fortibus,*
> *cum erit omnia Deus in omnibus.*

> O what their joy and their glory must be,
> Those endless sabbaths the blessed ones see;
> Crown for the valiant, to weary ones rest:
> God shall be all, and in all ever blest.
>
> (Peter Abelard; translation by J. M. Neale)

We too, therefore, will live endless sabbaths out of our death in him. When the weariness of all our living is over, we shall receive the reward of our faithfulness unto death (Rev. 2:10). The Lamb Slain (5:6, 9, 12; 13:8), who makes all things new (21:5), will give us the crown of his eternal life (2:10).

Item: The personal significance of the Christian celebration of Holy Saturday—of the Holy Sabbath. What we celebrate is precisely *death,* not dying. *Dying,* if you think about it, is simply the world's worst way of *living:* it is tag-end living, minimal living, hardly living. And dying, besides being no fun, is also totally unfruitful: nothing grows out of it because the common reaction to it is a continuous attempt, physically and mentally, to *reverse* it—to go counter to the direction that the universe in this particular instance wants to take. But death, precisely because it is an arrival at an accomplished fact, and above all because Jesus rises gloriously out of that fact, is the most fruitful thing there is. Death, therefore—nothingness, *no thing*—is the *only thing* we need.

Item: Nothingness. On Holy Saturday, the Holy Sabbath, the Easter Vigil begins in a darkened church. The symbolism is obvious: we are dead in Christ's death. But then, in honor of the resurrection, the new fire is struck, the paschal candle is lit, and we begin the celebration of a new creation out of the nothingness of death. People often say they are afraid of death—about, as they sometimes put it, having to be *nothing* after all these lovely years of being *something.* When they tell me that, I try to focus the problem more tightly. "Let me see if I understand you," I say. "You're bothered by the thought that you will be non-existent in, say, the year 2075. But tell me something. Has it ever occurred to you to worry about the fact that you were likewise non-existent in 1875? Of course it hasn't: for the simple reason that, by the forces of nature alone, you got bravely over that first attack of nothingness and were born. Well, all the Gospel is telling you is that your death—your second bout of nothingness—is going to be even less of a problem than your first. By the power of Jesus' death and resurrection, you will get bravely over that too, and be reborn. In fact, you already have been; so go find something more dangerous to worry about."

Final Item: Only death is usable in the new creation. Jesus came to raise the dead. He did not come to raise the living; and he especially did not come to raise the dying (remember Lazarus: John 11:1-16).

As long as you and I are just hanging onto life, Jesus cannot do a thing for us. He saves the dead, not the moribund; the lost, not the detoured; the last, not the middle of the line. It is only when we go all the way into death—past living and past dying—that we can experience his power.

I have already dealt (in *The Parables of the Kingdom*) with the parables of the Mustard Seed and of the Yeast as Mark and Matthew locate them in the earlier part of Jesus' ministry. All I am going to offer here are a few reflections based on the fact that in Luke (Luke 13:18-21; Aland nos. 209-210) Jesus tells these parables a second time during his final journey to Jerusalem. A mustard seed, or any seed for that matter, must end its career as a seed before something can come of it. It must, that is, go all the way into death. Therefore, while Luke's placement of this parable may be singular, there is nonetheless a certain thematic appropriateness about it: Jesus, too, must end his career before anything can come of his messianic program.

One other observation on the mustard seed: it becomes a tree *(déndron)*. I think it worth noting that the imagery of the tree is not only central to the shape of the Scripture but also inseparably involved with death. Mankind falls into sin and death by a tree in Genesis, is saved by a tree through the death of the Incarnate Lord on the cross, and lives forever in the New Jerusalem in the shade of the tree of life that yields twelve fruits and whose leaves are for the healing of the nations. True enough, the Greek word for "tree" in these instances is *xýlon,* not *déndron:* it means "wood"—originally, lumber or firewood. But in the later Greek of the New Testament, it quite plainly means "tree" ("*xýlon* of life," for example, Rev. 22:2); and from that usage, it easily becomes a metonym for the cross: Jesus "hung upon a *xýlon*" (Acts 5:30) and "bore our sins on the *xýlon*" (1 Pet. 2:24), etc.

About the yeast *(zýmē),* only one comment. While yeast cannot be said to die when it is mixed into dough, it can legitimately be said to get lost in the mixture. Jesus, in fact, says that the woman "hid" it *(enékrypsen)* in three measures of flour. Consequently, even though the yeast is not an image of death, it is nonetheless an image of the saving lostness that Jesus, at this juncture, talks about almost as much as he does about death (see the Good Samaritan, for example—and especially the upcoming parables in Luke 15: the Lost Sheep, the Lost Coin, the Lost Son).

For the present, however, Luke proceeds to the parable of the Narrow Door (Luke 13:22-30; Aland no. 211)—but not without a reminder (verse 22) that Jesus is saying all these things precisely on his way to Jerusalem. For both Luke and Jesus, in other words, death hangs over this entire proceeding; to me, therefore, the verse is yet another justification for my use of death as the touchstone of the parables of grace.

Someone comes up to Jesus on the road and says to him, "Lord *[kýrie],* will only a few be saved?" In one sense, it is easy to understand how such a presumption of exclusivity could arise in the questioner's mind, considering the harsh-sounding, apparently judgmental parables he may have heard during this journey: the Good Samaritan, the Friend at Midnight, the Sign of Jonah, the Rich Fool, the Watchful Servants, the Barren Fig Tree. On the other hand, it must have been exasperating to Jesus to have his main point so completely missed: he was, after all, laying down a program of salvation (namely, faith in his death and resurrection) that would make eternal life available to absolutely everybody—and on a giveaway basis at that. "All you have to do is be dead and trust in my death," he said in effect; "I do all the rest."

Jesus' difficulty, of course, was that such a program was simply unintelligible to his hearers. As every preacher knows, people hear not what is said but only what they are prepared to hear. Consequently, since no one in Jesus' audience (the disciples included) was in any way prepared to comprehend the idea of a Messiah who would die, it is not surprising that his parabolic intimations of his death and resurrection—not to mention his literal prediction of it—went totally unheard.

Accordingly, Jesus' hearers fastened their minds on something they could at least partially grasp, namely, the notes of judgment and even of condemnation in his parables of grace; and they skipped blithely over death and resurrection by which alone grace works. And Jesus himself (who by no means had the world's longest fuse) seems simply to have become monumentally annoyed with them. Almost out of spite, he gives no direct answer to the question of whether only a few will be saved. Instead, he deliberately perpetuates their confusion by giving his answer in the ham-fistedly judgmental imagery of the Narrow Door. It is a prime example of Jesus positively encouraging misunderstanding.

Straight off, he responds in the plural, thus answering his questioner by playing to the crowd: "Strive *[agōnízesthe]* to enter through the narrow door *[stenḗs thýras]*." What he is doing, of course, is the old rhetorical trick of setting up a straw man by confirming the worst case. Because insofar as an eschatology maven like his questioner could hear him at all, the only thing Jesus could possibly mean by "striving" and "narrow door" would be, "You bet there'll be only a few, sonny; and if you're smart, you'll knock yourself out studying for the entrance exam. Because I've made it so tough that most of you are going to flunk."

I realize, of course, that there are a fair number of Christian preachers who would be more than happy to stand up and say that's exactly what Jesus meant. But I have trouble with such a failure to spot the irony Jesus is using here. So much so, that when I put their cheerfully exclusivist interpretation of his words against something like John 12:32 ("I, if I be lifted up, will draw *all [pántas]* to me"), the circuit breakers in my mind simply pop. And by the same token, when I put that dire interpretation against what I think Jesus is actually saying in these parables of grace, I am forced to look for another, more catholic interpretation of the Narrow Door.

So here it is. The narrow door—the tight squeeze in front of absolutely free salvation—is faith in Jesus' death. Jesus does not set up ten thousand tricky wickets and threaten to admit to heaven only the aces who can negotiate every one of them. Jesus has simply put, smack in the front of his Father's house of many mansions, the one, scant doorway of his death and ours. Its forbidding narrowness lies not in the fact that it is so small it is hard to find; rather it lies in the fact that it is so repulsive it is hard to accept. Let me, in all reverence, repeat the last assertion as plainly as possible: to anyone in his right mind, the program of salvation via death, as proposed by Jesus, simply stinks on ice. It lets in the riffraff, since all they have to be is dead; and it offends the classy, since they wouldn't even be caught dead entertaining such a proposition. Besides, in Gethsemane, Jesus himself said it was a terrible idea and he warned us over and over again that the number of people who would be willing to buy it would be undamned few. He did not, however, say either that it was his heart's desire that the number actually be few, or that he was going to sit up in his private tower cheering every time somebody turned away in disgust from such a forbidding front door. In fact, he says that he himself, hanging dead on the cross, *is* the front door ("I am the door," John 10:9); and far from turning up his nose at the world's rejection, he insists on trying forever to convert it to acceptance—"I, if I be lifted up from the earth, will draw all to myself" (John 12:32).

Do you see what that does for the details of this parable? It abolishes the exclusivity of the imagery of narrowness and makes the parable susceptible of an inclusive interpretation. Watch. All the suction in the universe—all the "drawing" by which the Word woos creation back to be his bride—is through the narrow door of death. You may run from it, you may fight it, you may protest it, you may hate it—all in the name of what you call life. But if ever just once you slip up in your frantic struggle to live your way to your eternal home—if just once you simply drop dead—well then, sssslurrrp!!! . . . the suction will get you, and home you go. Not because you deserve to; only because that's the way the universe is built. Good Friday and the Holy Sabbath are the tip of the iceberg of redeeming death that lies under all of history. It was the Lamb Slain *from the foundation of the world* (Rev. 13:8) who said, "I, if I be lifted up, will draw all to me."

Salvation is hard, therefore, and salvation is easy—and the hardest thing about it is its easiness. It uses such cheap, low-down methods that only the last, the lost, the least, the little, and the dead will ever be able to cotton onto it. Moreover, that is exactly what Jesus says at the end of his introduction (Luke 13:24) to the parable of the Narrow Door: "For many, I tell you, will seek to enter and will not be able" (*ouk ischýsousin,* will not have the strength for it).

But then he takes a tack that seems to undo everything I have been saying—a tack that has given editors of the Greek text a punctuation problem. If you put—as most of them do—a full stop (that is, a period) after "will not be able" at the end of verse 24, then you put at least some distance between those words and the actual beginning of the parable in verse 25, to wit, "Once the master of the house has risen up and closed the door. . . ." In other words, you leave open the possibility that the inability to enter is not necessarily due solely—or even at all—to the master's closing of the door. But if you put a half stop (a comma, in this case) between the verses, then you have practically necessitated two conclusions: first, that the householder's door in verse 25 is the same as the narrow door in verse 24; and second, that the reason why only a few are ever going to make it to their final home is that our Lord and Master's idea of how to throw a good party is to keep out as many people as possible. Obviously, since I don't believe that the second conclusion is Gospel, and since I am convinced that the first is not the case, I myself am delighted to put a full stop after verse 24. (For the record, the KJV, RSV, NEB, NIV, and many others opt for the full stop. Examples of the effect of the half stop may be seen in the English Revised Version [marginal reading] and in J. B. Phillip's translation.) In any case, let me put a full stop to textual criticism and get back to what should probably now be called the parable of the Narrow Door versus the Other Door.

Jesus says: "Once the householder *[oikodespótēs]* has risen up *[egerthẹ̑]* and closed the door *[thýran]*, you will begin to stand outside and knock *[kroúein]* on the door saying, 'Lord, open up for us'; and he will answer and say to you, 'I don't know where you're coming from.' Then you will begin to say, 'We ate and drank right in front of you and you taught in our streets.' And he will say to you again, 'I don't know where you're coming from; get away from me, all you workers of iniquity.'"

Far enough for the moment. Look carefully at the words I have given the Greek for. *Oikodespótēs* (I am shifting to the milder translation, "householder") is a word that has appeared before and will appear again. Jesus uses it twice during the parables of the kingdom (see my previous volume, *The Parables of the Kingdom*): once in referring to the householder in the parable of the Wheat and the Weeds (Matt. 13:24-30)—which householder, please note, was the very one who said *áphes* (forgive, let them be) concerning the weeds; and he uses it a second time in referring to the householder who "brings forth out of his treasure things new and old" (Matt. 13:51-52)—the one whom Jesus holds up as a model for the instructed disciple. He also applies the word to three other significant characters: to the lord of the vineyard, the gracious Christ-figure in the parable of the Laborers in the Vineyard (Matt. 20:1-16); to the party-giver in the parable of the Great Supper (Luke 14:15-24) who goes to heroic lengths to fill his house with guests; and perhaps most remarkably, to the figure of God the Father in the parable of the Vineyard and the Tenants (Matt. 21:33-44)—that is, to the vineyard owner whose son was killed for the sake of the vineyard. (The

Vulgate, incidentally, translates *oikodespótēs* as *paterfamilias* in all these instances—thus suggesting, whether in the case of Christ-figure or Father-figure, the desirability of a familial, rather than a coldly judicial, interpretation.)

In the light of all these usages, what can be said about the force of *oikodespótēs* in the parable of the Doors? I think it has the effect of making this a parable about the divine housekeeping—about the way God provides for and manages the whole house of creation—about (to use the correct theological term) the divine *economy*. And it implies that while the managing of his house may well require certain exclusionary measures, those measures are not the divine *oikodespótēs'* idea of how to run a home. In short, I think it only fair to import into the interpretation of this parable all the freight of grace and leniency carried by the word *oikodespótēs* in Jesus' other parables. Accordingly, I am going to take the householder here not only as a Christ-figure but also as a figure of some gentleness. I am not at all disposed to follow the usual interpretation and make him out to be a tough customer.

Two factors lead me to take that approach: the general thrust of the imagery of the parable, and the specific presence of the words *egerthę̄* (has risen) and *thýran* (door). Consider the significance of the imagery first.

What Jesus is doing here is very like what he did in the parable of the Friend at Midnight: he is painting a parabolic picture, using nighttime behavior as his model. But in this case, he prefaces his parable with the apparently forbidding image of a narrow door. That image, though, is by no means an entirely negative one. Unless we are going to make Jesus out to be a trickster daring us to do the impossible, this first door he speaks of must be seen as an unlocked door, a usable door, an open door. Nevertheless, when he begins the parable itself in verse 25, he seems to confuse the imagery: he sketches a picture of a householder getting up and *closing* a door. As I said, my way of resolving the confusion is to conclude that he is talking about two different doors; otherwise, what would be the point of his telling us to strive to enter what he has slammed shut? Actually, I don't think there is any real confusion here at all: I think that Jesus used the word "door" in verse 24 as a variant of "gate" (see Matt. 7:13-14—the "narrow" imagery could well have been repeat-ed many times by Jesus, with occasional alterations for variety's sake). But then, I think, his use of the word "door" suggested—on the analogy of the Friend at Midnight—the possibility of yet another parable.

In any case, the picture seems to me to be as follows. It is evening, after supper. The householder has been reading *The Wall Street Journal* or watching the ten o'clock news, and he has fallen asleep in his recliner. Suddenly the clock strikes midnight. He awakes with a jolt, realizes the time, *gets up (egerthé),* and does all the things he should have done earlier. He locks the door *(thýran),* turns off the lights, and goes to his proper bed. But on his way to some solid sleep at last, he is interrupted by insistent banging on his front door: a mob of people, claiming to be his friends, want to come in and to . . . well, what might they want to do? Go to bed with him and sleep the whole night? Hardly. Jesus postulates far too hyper a crowd for such quiet behavior. Perhaps what they want is a chance to bend his ear with the latest gossip, or perhaps just a chance to prove to the neighbors they are important enough to be let into his house any hour of the day or night. Whatever it is, it will be something based entirely on *their* concerns, *their* convenience, their problems—in short on *their lives.* At any rate, as Jesus portrays them, they talk like a bunch of selfish parvenus: after the householder's first snub, they come back at him with indignation disguised as bonhomie. "But we've *lunched* with you! We've had *drinks* with you at the club! We've even attended your *fabulous* lectures!" Despite their social-climbing cajolery, though, Jesus has the householder tell them they simply don't fit in with his plans: "I don't know where you're coming from," he says. For all he can understand of their idiotic lives and preoccupations they might as well be from another planet. They certainly haven't the foggiest notion of how *he* wants to operate.

Now then. Having thus extrapolated the parable, let me exegete my extrapolation. The *nap* out of which the householder/Christ-figure rises is Jesus' three days in the tomb. The *door* he closes is the door to the exchanges of ordinary living. And the *sleep* to which he finally goes is the endless sabbath of the death of Jesus, which is the perpetual basis of the resurrection to eternal life.

And what, at that rate, is the *narrow door* the householder has still left open? Well, it is the remote possibility that, instead of noisily insisting on their own notions of living their way to salvation, they might just join him in the silence of his death and wait in faith for resurrection.

Is that forcing the original text? On balance, I don't think so. But even if it is, I'm not worried: no one ever gets through Scripture without occasionally putting the arm on one passage in favor of another. Accordingly, because I really do think the *oikodespótēs* is a Christ-figure—and because I really don't think Jesus will ever close the door of grace—I think the closing of the *oikodespótēs'* door should be interpreted not as the locking out of the damned but as the closing of the door of ordinary living as a way to eternal life. Jesus our *oikodespótēs* rises out of his three-day nap in the grave and he closes all other doors to salvation except faithful waiting in the endless sabbath of his death. He leaves us, that is, no entrance into life but the narrow door of our own nothingness and death—the Door, in fact (John 10:9), that is Jesus himself.

Please note carefully what I am saying. I am not saying there is no such thing in Scripture as God's slamming the door on the damned: there is plenty of it, and I am not about to say that he won't, in the end, do something awfully similar. (I might, of course, make a few qualifications about the subject—I might even be accused of qualifying the hell right out of it. But yes, Virginia: if you have to know, I really do think there is a hell.) What I *am* saying is that this parable of the Door is not one of the places where the final disposition of the damned is being talked about. For my money, it is yet another grace parable in judgment clothing—a phenomenon we have seen much of already, and will see more of in the parable of the Great Supper. And as with all such parables, it should be interpreted as gracefully as possible; it should not be used as an excuse to preach sermons on the tight security of the eschatological slammer.

What confirms me in that opinion is the fourth of the Greek words I have flagged, namely, *kroúein*, to knock. In the Book of Revelation (3:20), Jesus says, "Behold, I stand at the door and knock" *(kroúō)*. Do you see what that says about this parable? It says that while all the world's winners are out there knocking their knuckles bloody on the locked doors of their lives, Jesus is knocking quietly at the narrow door of their deaths trying to get them to let him in. It says, in other words, the exact opposite of what most people think: not that he is busy dreaming up ways to keep sinners out but that he is actively and forever committed to *letting himself in*.

(Don't worry, Virginia, that still leaves you a terrific hell: if they never open up and he never stops knocking, that's the hell of it all.) It says, in short, that this is a parable of grace, even though it manages to be that only by the desperate expedient of demanding to be stood on its head.

One last point before proceeding. The parallels between this parable and the Friend at Midnight (Luke 11:5-13) are worth noting. In both, there is a door *(thýran)* that has been closed by the householder—who in the case of the Friend at Midnight says also, "my children *[paidía]* are with me in bed; I cannot rise *[anastás]* to give you anything." In the light of where we have come in this book, that seems to me to say that God's real children—those who trust only in Jesus, who is the *paída* whom God raised *(anastás:* see Acts 3:26)—are with him in the bed of Jesus' endless death. And it says that Jesus will never get out of that bed, since it alone is the root of his resurrection. Nevertheless, there is definitely a rising in the Friend at Midnight. Though the householder in that case "will not rise *[anastás]* and give to him because he is his friend [that is, because of the merits of ordinary living], still, because of his shamelessness [his acceptance of his death as the only thing he's got], he will rise *[egertheís]* and give him as much as he needs [that is, life abundant in the resurrection]." Finally, the verb *kroúein,* to knock, also appears in the Friend at Midnight—but with the reverse assurance that our knocking will not be in vain. For this knocking is not the clamor of those trying respectably to live their way to salvation; rather it is the shameless, faithful acceptance of Jesus in his death as the Way, the Truth, and the Life. It is a knocking at God's door with nothing more to commend us than the Door himself, the dead Christ on the cross.

To return to the parable of the Narrow Door, then, Jesus continues by having the householder say (after the second "I don't know where you're coming from"): "get away from me, all you workers of iniquity. There will be weeping and gnashing of teeth when you see Abraham, Issac, and Jacob in the kingdom of God, and you yourselves thrown out of it. People will come from east and west and from north and south and they will sit down to eat *[anaklithésontai]* in the kingdom of God. And behold, those who are now last will be first and those who are now first will be last."

This is the summation of the parable. Jesus says that those who are knocking at the door of ordinary, plausible, right-handed living—all of them, mind you, "good" people trying to live decently—are nothing but workers of iniquity *(adikías)*, that is, of the unrighteousness that springs from unfaith. Good living is no more capable of justifying us than bad living is of condemning us. Only faith in Jesus dead and risen has anything to do with the case. And Jesus drives that home by citing specific examples of faith—of blind, even stupid, obedience to the God who works by raising the dead. He holds up Abraham, Isaac, Jacob, and the prophets and he says that they will be the ones who are in the kingdom, while all the types who are trying to climb their way into the eternal social register will be out in the cold.

Finally, though, he says something that I think vindicates the frankly catholic interpretation I have given the Narrow Door. He says that people (the Greek simply says "they") will come from all over creation and sit down *at supper*—which means, as I read it in the light of the finished imagery of Scripture, at nothing less than the *Marriage Supper of the Lamb*. That imagery suggests not a trickle of guests who, after heroic efforts, will find their way to some slow leak of a house party, but a flood of billions upon billions who—free, for nothing—will be drawn by the love of Jesus into the ultimate wedding blowout. True enough, they will be drawn through strait gates and narrow ways; but they will be drawn by the Narrow Door himself, and they will be drawn inexorably. All they need is the willingness to be last—and lost and least and little and dead—for by his grace upon their deaths, they will be first in the resurrection of the dead.

CHAPTER TWELVE

Death and the Party

The Transition to the Great Banquet

Fascinatingly—considering in particular that Jesus at this point is consciously and deliberately on his way to death—the fourteenth and fifteenth chapters of Luke (Aland nos. 214-221) have, as their principal motif, the image of the party. Chapter 14 begins with a sit-down dinner in the home of a leading Pharisee—a dinner at which Jesus does a number of bizarre things: he performs an unacceptable healing on the sabbath, he criticizes his fellow guests' social behavior, he dispenses odd, if not nonsensical, advice on party-giving, and he tops off the occasion by confusing everyone with the parable of the Great Banquet. In the rest of the chapter, he lectures the crowds that follow him on the cost of the paradoxical "party" he is about to give the world in his death and resurrection; and in chapter 15, he regales us with no fewer than three parties: one each for the Lost Sheep, the Lost Coin, and the Lost Son. All in all, he clearly links the theme of the party, both explicitly and implicitly, with the mystery of death, lastness, and lostness that he has been adumbrating all through this final journey to Jerusalem.

This combining of "death-talk" with party imagery is not uncommon in Scripture (to recall only the climactic instance of it, think of the Marriage Supper of the Lamb Slain in the final chapters of Revelation). But it occurs most frequently as a twist that Jesus gives to certain of his parables. He has already included a wedding reception in the parable of the Watchful Servants, and he has introduced the notion of an eschatological dinner party at the end of the parable of the Narrow Door. And in the Prodigal Son and the King's Son's Wedding, he will make a completely literal connection

117

between death/lastness and the party. But before moving on to the parties at hand in Luke 14, I want to say a few words about the material at the end of chapter 13 that forms the bridge to them.

Immediately after he has told the parable of the Narrow Door, some of the Pharisees warn Jesus to get out of town: Herod, they tell him, wants to kill him. This is crocodile solicitousness on their part, of course: they themselves have been after Jesus' scalp for almost as long as he has been preaching (since Mark 3:6, in fact). Nor does Jesus respond in any worried way to their rattling of his cage. He is on his way to Jerusalem for the express purpose of being killed; his first reaction to their fake concern, therefore, boils down to little more than a snappish "So what?" "Go and tell that fox," he says, "'Look, I cast out demons and do cures today and tomorrow, and on the third day I shall finish my work [*teleioúmai*, be brought to my completion: coupled as it is here with "the third day" the word is a clear reference to Jesus' death]. Still, I have to continue on my way today, tomorrow, and the next day, because it is not fitting for a prophet to be killed outside of Jerusalem'" (Luke 13:32-33).

But Jesus' snappishness changes abruptly to tenderness and pity. At the thought of his own death—and in particular, I suppose, of its radical unrecognizability as a messianic act—he laments over the Holy City which he now knows will not accept him. "O Jerusalem, Jerusalem, killing the prophets and stoning those sent to you! How often would I have gathered your children together as a hen gathers her chicks under her wings, and you would not! Behold, your house is taken away from you. [The Greek verb behind 'taken away' is, once again, the multivalent *aphiénai*: forgive, permit, let be, leave, forsake, let go, dismiss, divorce.] And I tell you, you will not see me until the time comes when you say, 'Blessed is he who comes in the name of the Lord!'"

I find this whole passage to be a vindication of my insistence on using death as a touchstone for the interpretation of the parables of grace. It shows quite clearly how close to the surface of Jesus' mind the subject really was. All it took was one mention of Herod's antipathy (just a little political gossip, really, with a nasty edge to it) and out came a flood of messianic utterances couched in relentless death-talk. And the specific words he uses make the death-resurrection character of his messiahship plainer than ever. "Today and tomorrow," he says (that is, for the time being, for now, for the time before the mystery is revealed—for the time, if you will, of the *signs* of his messianic program rather than of the *program* itself), "I cast out demons and do cures" (in other words, he acts like a recognizable, interventionist Messiah); "and on the third day [*tȩ̄ trítȩ̄ hēmérą:* as noted, these words are a clear reference to resurrection out of death; compare, for example, Matt. 16:21 and parallels; Mark 9:31 and parallels; Luke 18:33 and parallels] I shall finish my work" (*teleioúmai:* be perfected, that is, bring my actual messianic program, and not just the signs of it, to accomplishment—compare the use of the same verb by Jesus on the cross in John 19:30: *tetélestai,* "it is finished").

So too, I find the imagery of his lament over Jerusalem vindicative of my interpretation. Jerusalem deals out death but will not accept a Messiah who works by death. Jesus has longed to gather his people under his wings in love; but now the only way he will accomplish that is by the very death they will inflict upon him. They will be healed by his stripes; death and not living will be the instrument of their salvation. The net effect of all the plausible, right-handed schemes the city has concocted in the name of living has not been life, it has been the corruption of life—and it will very shortly be nothing less than disaster. And as with Jerusalem, so with us. The human race's efforts to get its act together have resulted in many things, a lot of them plain, unvarnished messes; but the one thing we have never succeeded in doing is getting our act together. And therefore for us, as for Jerusalem, the house of our life—the ramshackle agglomeration of bright ideas, old stupidities, good intentions, and ill will in which we have for so long tried to live our way to some semblance of wholeness—is put away from us, divorced from us, set permanently out of our reach. The only home left for us now is Jesus' death.

Far from being a tragedy, though, this divorce, this *áphesis,* this separation from the house of our own life is, by the very word Jesus uses, an absolution for all the failings of that house. *"Aphíetai hymín ho oíkos hymṓn,"* he says. In a good half of its many uses in the New Testament, the verb *aphiénai* means simply *forgive;* accordingly, this *áphesis* is not just the loss of our life, it is also, by a great mercy, the loss of the garbage of our life. All the clutter that, like decrepit bachelors, we have allowed to pile up in the house of our living, all the hates, the lies, the lusts, and the lunacies—the whole lifetime's accumulation of irretrievable mistakes—has been forgiven, absolved, put away, carted off.

If then we accept that absolution, that housecleaning that is a house-removal—and if we take up residence in the clean emptiness of Jesus' death—we will have his life and have it abundantly. But if we try to hang onto the old house of our living we will have only hell. Because that Collier brothers' mansion, that Charles Addams monstrosity, is *gone*. *We are dead,* and our life is hid with Christ in God (Col. 3:3). To go back to that life is to go back to nothing. The only real dwelling we have now is the Father's house of many mansions: hell is simply the stupid pretense that *nowhere* really would be a nicer place to spend eternity.

But enough of the bridge to Luke 14; time to let a whole series of parties begin. Jesus goes to the house of a certain Pharisee to have dinner on the sabbath day . . . but since you probably know this story of healing on the sabbath in its straight form, let me try to make it more accessible by updating a few details. Imagine a modern house for this prosperous Pharisee—one with a dining room grand enough to hold a fourteen-foot table. Make the meal to which he invited Jesus a sit-down dinner for twelve; and make the guests Episcopalians or Presbyterians—pleasant but a bit shirty is the effect you want. Then bring on Jesus.

He gets through the soup and the fish well enough, but just as the roast is brought in, he discovers that the gentleman next to him has a back problem. Being not only kindhearted but good with his hands (perhaps he has studied Healing Touch at a holistic health center), he suddenly decides to help the man, right there in front of everybody. "May I have your attention just a minute, folks?" he says. "Old Waldo here has a real bad back. Hurts him worse than a toothache. So if it's okay with you all, I'm just going to plop him down right here on the dinner table and do a little healing on him. Er, Mrs. Terwilliger, do you think you could move that roast down to the other end? Waldo's a pretty big old boy, you know. There! Up you go now, Waldo. And mind your feet so you don't get your shoelaces in the cauliflower."

Do you see? The crime of healing on the sabbath is no mere technical violation of the law. It is a crime against civility, against decency, against common sense—against, in short, the received wisdom about how life should be lived. It is proof that the person who commits it has lost all sense of conformity and manners and is therefore dangerously impervious to the glue that holds everybody else's life together. And Jesus' curing of the man's dropsy at a sabbath dinner is as alarming as the hypothetical treatment of old Waldo in the midst of the Limoges: normal people would "rather die" than do, or even watch, something like that—they would be, as they say revealingly, "mortified." Therefore when anyone actually does behave that way, what alarms them is precisely the appearance, in the midst of all their fearful living, of someone who has been liberated from the fear of death.

Jesus, of course, challenges his host and fellow guests to accept his liberation. He asks them "Is it lawful to heal on the sabbath or not?" But as with Waldo, he doesn't bother to wait for an answer. When he's done with the healing—during and after which all present have bitten their tongues and uttered not one complaining word about such an imposition—he gets up on his high horse and criticizes them for *thinking* he's a boor. His words, "Which of you, if his son or his ox falls into a pit, will not pull him out on the sabbath day?" are in about as good taste as would be, "Well, Waldo's just fine now, but don't any of you dare start thinking unkindly of me for fixing him up, because you'd do exactly the same thing, if your child or your favorite dog came in here all smashed and bloody."

Jesus' behavior, you see, is simply unpardonable: besides being tasteless, it presumes his fellow guests are worse than they are. Nobody present wants him *not* to heal the sick. They simply can't understand why he has to turn the healing into a sideshow of bad manners. What they are probably thinking is something quite mild—like, "Oh, come now; heal all you like, but can't you make us all just a bit more comfortable and put off the actual treatment till after dinner?" The scribes and Pharisees, you see, are being neither unreasonable nor heartless. What time, after all, was the sabbath meal? Noon? One? Three-thirty? *Tops,* all they're asking Jesus to do is wait six hours: the sabbath ends at sundown, for crying out loud! After that he can turn Waldo into Superman, for all they care. But the fact that he has to do it right now on the sabbath, between dinner and dessert, with Waldo's feet in the host's face, means only one thing: loony or sane, Jesus is bad news. Either way, he's just too unafraid to be safe company.

Which brings us to Jesus' side of the question. He did a good deal of healing on the sabbath. You might even say that healing on the sabbath was his favorite way of livening up an observance he felt had been unnecessarily toned down by the scribes and Pharisees. But there was more to it than that. Jesus was unique; and he perceived his uniqueness with increasing clarity as his life went on. The trouble with uniqueness, though, is that practically no one can see it as anything but craziness. All they see when they meet somebody truly one-of-a-kind is the electric sign inside their own heads that keeps flashing, "Not Like Us! Not Like Us!" Therefore, since one of Jesus' main points was that his method of salvation (namely, death and resurrection) would be like nothing any sane person could have a kind word for, he probably figured that healing on the sabbath was as good a way as any to introduce the world to its, and his, uniqueness.

In any case, healing on the sabbath is just as repugnant to the church nowadays as it was to the scribes and Pharisees in Jesus' time. Furthermore, if we insist on emulating him by doing a bit of it on our own, we will find ourselves just as despised and rejected as he was. Some modern instances of this aversion to healing on the sabbath? Helen decides she wants to start an AIDS support group in the local church. Response? "Well sure, Helen, sick people need help. But these guys are *queer!* We've got to think of the young kids. Better try someplace else." Or: Cynthia, drunk, calls her pastor at 3:00 A.M. and wants to talk about the problems she has with men. Response? "Now listen, Cynthia. I know this all seems very important to you right now, but: you woke me up out of a sound sleep; you've kept me on the phone for an hour; and now my wife is sitting next to me with smoke coming out of her ears because I'm being nice to another woman at four in the morning. I'm going to unplug the phone, Cynthia. I promise I'll call you, but I just have to get some sleep." Or finally, consider the pastor who divorces his wife, marries his mistress, and then suggests to the Official Board of the church that their allowing him to remain in the pulpit would be a splendid example of grace and forgiveness in action. Response? "No way, Jose."

But back to the text. Having offended everybody in sight by his willingness to toss aside the conventions of living—having given them, that is, a whiff of the freedom of death in the prison of their days—he finds himself on a roll. Not content with giving them a mere hint, he tells a parable that flings open every window in the jailhouse. Having noted how this crowd of snobs has clucked and sniffed about the seating arrangements, he begins, "When you are invited by someone to a wedding reception, don't sit down in the best place, because somebody more important than you may have been invited by your host. And then the host will have to come and say, 'Give your place to this man,' and you will be ashamed and have to sit in the lowest [*éschaton*, last] place. Instead, when you are invited, go and sit in the lowest [*éschaton*] place, so that when your host comes he will say to you, 'Come on up, friend, to a higher place'; then there will be honor [*dóxa*, glory] for you in the presence of all those who sit at the table with you. For everyone who exalts himself will be humbled and he who humbles himself will be exalted."

Unfortunately, that last line always manages to cast a pall over the rest of the parable. People hear "humble yourself" and they immediately think of the bitter pill of moral effort. But this parable is not about a cure that is worse than the disease; it's about the liberating joy that comes from letting the party happen instead of trying to put personal body English all over it. It's about, in other words, the "letting go" of Jesus himself who "for the joy that was set before him, endured the cross, despised the shame, and is set down on the right hand of God" (Heb. 12:2).

That connection between humility and death is reinforced by the symbolism of the entire parable. For insofar as we insist on taking what we have decided is the best place, we effectively close ourselves to all the other places at the table. It's like the illustration of the hand in chapter ten above: clutch the gift that you have in your palm at the moment and no other gifts can get in; hold it in a dead hand, though—in a flat, open hand—and the dance of gifts can proceed unimpeded. But note, too, how this parable expands that image. Jesus tells us that in life, as at the dinner table, we are to take the lowest seat. As already noted, the word used here for "lowest" is actually *éschatos,* the Greek for "last." That suggests, accordingly, that the precise seat we are invited into, the seat specifically reserved for each one of us, is death. For not only is death our last and lowest state but it is also the state that is the sole condition of our resurrection. Jesus speaks often of "the last day" *(hē eschátē hēméra)* as the day of resurrection and the day of judgment; here he simply develops the same theme.

Look next, though, at the Christ-figure in this parable. Obviously, it is the host; but notice how the image of host here is refracted and reflected by other places in Scripture. First, just as the host is the source of the invitation to the wedding, so Jesus calls the whole world to the Marriage Supper of the Lamb. "Go out into the highways and hedges," he says, "and *compel* them to come in" (Luke 14:23); "I, if I be lifted up from the earth, will draw *all* to me" (John 12:32). Second, with Jesus as with the host, whatever judgment is issued, favorable or unfavorable, it is issued precisely upon people who are *already guests*—that is, who have already been *invited into* and *accepted at* the party. Their right to be members of the party is never in doubt; only their acceptance of it is questioned. Finally, the host pronounces *favorable* judgment on those who accept the last and lowest place—namely, death—and who are willing to wait there for the fulfillment of his promise (John 6:39-40), "I will raise him up *[anastḗsō autón]* at the last day." (The resurrection, incidentally, is at least hinted at by the *aná* [up] words of the host in the parable, "Friend, come up higher": *prosanábēthi anṓteron.*)

One last verbal connection in this parable: I find in the phrase "with shame" (verse 9) an echo of the parable of the Friend at Midnight. Here as there we are told that death and loss rather than life and success are the instruments of our salvation. For if we hope to be saved by our talent for lifting ourselves into first place by our own bootstraps, then we will, by the very impossibility of the enterprise, "begin with shame *[aischýnēs]*" to take the lowest place—that is, to have lastness, lostness, and death thrust upon us without our acceptance. But if we are shameless enough to accept death as the instrument of our salvation—if, with a shamelessness *(anaídeian)* like that of the friend who came as a beggar at midnight, we will drop our pretenses of success and come to Jesus in our failure—then Jesus our Friend will rise, and Jesus our Host will come, and he will raise us up at the last day and bid the endless party to begin.

Meanwhile, however, Jesus continues to add to the tension of the party by criticizing his host as well: he suggests that the Pharisee who gave the dinner should not have invited the successful, healthy, competent guests who are present; rather he should have invited the poor, the maimed, the halt, and the blind.

It is easy to sympathize with the people who had to put up with Jesus—especially with this Pharisee who is only trying to have a decent sabbath meal. First it was Waldo on the table with the main course, then it was critical comments about his guests, and now it's a lecture about how he should have invited all the losers in town. Jesus was never even a candidate for the congeniality award. I have a theory that maybe he hung around with publicans and sinners because polite society found itself less and less interested in giving him houseroom.

On closer examination though, Jesus' remarks to his host are less personally attacking than they seem. He is at pains, as he has been all through his final journey to Jerusalem, to set forth death and lostness, not life and success, as the means of salvation. And at this dinner party he has found himself in the presence of a bunch of certified, solid-brass winners: establishment types who are positive they've got all the right tickets, religious and otherwise, and who think a fun evening consists of clawing your way to the top of the social heap. Therefore when he addresses his host, he is principally concerned to redress the imbalance he feels all around him, to assert once again his conviction that a life lived by winning is a losing proposition.

"When you give a luncheon or a dinner [*deípnon,* supper]," Jesus says to the Pharisee, "don't invite your friends or your brothers or your relatives or your rich neighbors, because they'll just reciprocate your invitation. But when you give a feast, invite the poor, the crippled, the lame, and the blind, and you will be blessed [*makários,* happy] because they don't have any way of paying you back. Rather, everything will be repaid to you in the resurrection [*anastásei*] of the just [*dikaíōn*]."

There are a number of ways of interpreting this passage; most of them, frankly, you can keep. If, for example, you take it as advice on how to run your social life, it is simply a formula for ruining an evening. Guests chosen only because they won't invite you to their house in return are less than likely to be scintillating dinner company. Alternatively, if you take it simply as an instance of oriental hyperbole—that is, if you interpret it as nothing more than a "don't forget the handicapped," phrased in the form of "don't waste your time on the healthy"—you reduce it to an unnecessarily complicated version of an ethical commonplace.

But as I take this text, I see in it yet another major theme poking its nose into the interpretative tent. Watch. Jesus has already been

critical of the following items taken from everybody's list of Favorite
Things To Be: Being First, Being Found, Being Big, Being Important, and Being Alive. Now however, he castigates the one item that
holds all these futilities together and gives them power over us,
namely, Being a Bookkeeper. The human race is positively addicted
to keeping records and remembering scores. What we call our "life"
is, for the most part, simply the juggling of accounts in our heads.
And yet, if God has announced anything in Jesus, it is that he,
for one, has pensioned off the bookkeeping department permanently.

It is bookkeeping, therefore—our enslavement to it and God's
rejection of it—that seems to me to be the burden of the closing
lines of this parable of the Chief Seats. Jesus warns his host not to
consult any records he has kept on people: not the Friend/Foe
ledger, not the Rich/Poor volume—and none of the other books
either; not Nice/Nasty, Winners/Losers, or even Good/Bad. And
he warns him because, as far as God is concerned, that way of doing
business is over. It may be our sacred conviction that the only way to
keep God happy, the stars in their courses, our children safe, our
psyches adjusted, and our neighbors reasonable is to be ready, at
every moment, to have the books we have kept on ourselves and
others audited. But that is not God's conviction because he has
taken away the handwriting that was against us (Col. 2:14). In
Jesus' death and resurrection, God has declared that he isn't the least
interested in examining anybody's books ever again, not even his
own: he's nailed them all to the cross. Accountability, however
much it may be a buzzword now, is not one of his eschatological
categories.

That, I take it, is the point of Jesus' words against reciprocation
and repayment. Jesus is saying, "Listen, you are absolutely mired in
your scorekeeping, bookkeeping lives. You are so busy trying to
hold the world together by getting your accounts straight that you
hardly have time to notice that it's falling apart faster than ever. Why
don't you just let go? Thumb your nose at the ledger! Drop dead to
the accounting! Because it's not just one more thing that can't save
you; it's the flypaper that catches everything else that can't save you
and leaves you stuck with it forever. Look, I'm on my way to Jerusalem to die so you can be saved, free for nothing. I'm going up there
to give you a dramatic demonstration of shutting up once and for all

on the subject of the divine bookkeeping. What's the point, then, of your keeping records when I'm not?"

Do you see? He who was sent not to judge the world but to save the world (John 3:17) *will not count our records against us*. What the Son will offer the Father at the last day is the silence of his death on the subject of our sins and the power of his resurrection on the subject of our life. Therefore we are to stop—right now—living as if we could have the least influence on that happy outcome by fussing about who owes what to whom. That, if you will, is why Jesus tells his host to invite people who can't invite him back: to get him to stop doing everything in his life on the basis of debit and credit and to open his eyes to the way God does business. Jesus says to him: "Forget about making a social buck by inviting the right people—and forget about making a spiritual buck by doing the right thing. Invite the wrong people! Do the wrong thing! You want to have a dinner party? Have a stupid dinner party! You want to have a life? Have a loser's life! Spit in the eye of the accounting department! Invite anybody you don't like and be anything you don't like; but don't for a minute mess with anything that isn't last, lost, least, little, and dead. Because that's where the action is, not in your Guinness Book of Spiritual Records."

At the end of his speech to the host, Jesus specifically ties this condemnation of bookkeeping to the resurrection. "You will be happy *[makários]*," he tells his host in verse 14, "precisely because these losers and deadbeats you invite won't be able to repay you." He says, in other words, that happiness can never come in until the bookkeeping stops, until the hand that clutches at the dance goes dead and lets the dance happen freely. And he says that the place where that happy consequence will burst upon us is at the resurrection *(en tę anastásei)* of the just *(dikaíōn)*. And the just, please note, are not stuffy, righteous types with yard-long lists of good works, but simply all the forgiven sinners of the world who live by faith—who just trust Jesus and laugh out loud at the layoff of all the accountants.

And the unjust? Well, the unjust are all the forgiven sinners of the world who, stupidly, live by unfaith—who are going to insist on showing up at the resurrection with all their record books, as if it were an IRS audit. The unjust are the idiots who are going to try to talk Jesus into checking his bookkeeping against theirs. And do you know what Jesus is going to say to them—what, for example, he will say to his host if he comes to the resurrection with such a request? I think he will say, "Just forget it, Arthur. I suppose we have those books around here somewhere, and if you're really determined to stand in front of my great white throne and make an ass of yourself, I guess they can be opened (Rev. 20:12). Frankly, though, nobody up here pays any attention to them. What will happen will be that while you're busy reading and weeping over everything in those books, I will go and open my *other book* (Rev. 20:12, again), the book of life—the book that has in it the names of everybody I ever drew to myself by dying and rising. And when I open that book, I'm going to read out to the whole universe every last word that's written there. And you know what that's going to be? It's going to be just *Arthur.* Nothing else. None of your bad deeds, because I erased them all. And none of your good deeds, because I didn't count them, I just enjoyed them. So what I'll read out, Arthur, will be just *Arthur!* real loud. And my Father will smile and say, 'Hey, Arthur! You're just the way I pictured you!' And the universe will giggle and say, 'That's some Arthur you've got there!' But me, I'll just wink at you and say, 'Arthur, c'mon up here and plunk yourself down by my great white throne and let's you and me have a good long practice laugh before this party gets so loud we can't even hear how much fun we're having."

CHAPTER THIRTEEN

The Party Parables

The Great Banquet and the Prodigal Son

Meanwhile, back at Luke 14, the image of the party continues to dominate the proceedings. Jesus' next parable, the Great Banquet (Luke 14:15-24; Aland no. 216), is told at the very dinner table where he has been regaling everyone with his upside-down notions of what constitutes proper social behavior. But the parable of the Great Banquet does not simply arise out of that awkward meal; it also anticipates the festivities yet to come in chapter 15—in particular, the definitive party in the parable of the Prodigal Son. As a matter of fact, I think a case can be made that the Prodigal Son's perfect embodiment of what I have been calling the "grace" themes—its exaltation, for example, of losing over winning, its utter disdain for bookkeeping, its flatfooted references to death and resurrection, and, most notably, its celebration of them all with a blowout compared to which all previous parties look like slow leaks—made it, for Luke, the organizing principle of the entire sequence of passages in chapters 14 and 15.

Look at the evidence of the text. Much of what is included here appears nowhere else: the healing at the Pharisee's dinner party, the lecture to guests and host, and the parables of the Lost Coin and the Lost (Prodigal) Son are found only in Luke. The rest of the items, of course, appear in other Gospels as well. The Great Banquet, the lecture on the cost of discipleship, and the parable of the Tasteless Salt are found in Matthew; and the Lost Sheep is in Mark. But whereas in those Gospels these materials are scattered about in diverse contexts, in Luke their proximity to the story of the Prodigal Son makes their common themes fairly leap off the page. Consider. For one thing, there is a party in almost every one of them. For another, the last, the lost, and the dead are held up as God's chosen vessels. And for good measure, the first, the unstrayed, and the alive—all the best and brightest—are displayed as being in no way God's cup of tea. As far as I am concerned therefore, the parable of the Prodigal is the sun around which Luke has made the rest of these materials orbit.

On then with the Great Banquet, beginning with its relationship to the Prodigal Son. This story, about a man whose invited guests refuse to come to his party and who then pressgangs the riffraff of the town into filling up his house, appears twice in the Gospels: in Luke 14, where it occurs during the final journey to Jerusalem; and in Matthew 22, where it occurs between Palm Sunday and the crucifixion. By my classification, therefore, the Lukan version is a parable of grace and the Matthean one (the King's Son's Wedding), a parable of judgment. Moreover, the respective versions bear that out. As Jesus tells the parable in Luke, the governing consideration is the host's gracious desire that his house be filled. The note of judgment is struck only lightly: the host is angry when his invitations are refused and declares at the end that none of those who were invited will taste of his supper. By contrast, the story in Matthew is full of judgment, not to mention savagery: the invited guests murder the servants who bring the king's invitation; the king sends out his armies, destroys those murderers, and burns up their city (social life in this parable seems definitely more urgent than gracious); and at the end of the parable, the man without the wedding garment is cast into outer darkness. Therefore, leaving Jesus' telling of the story in its Matthean form for consideration in the forthcoming volume on the parables of judgment, let us look at the present, grace-oriented version in Luke.

Note how it begins. "When one of those who sat at table with him heard this [Jesus' discourse in Luke 14:1-14], he said to him, 'Blessed is he who shall eat bread in the kingdom of God!'" As I read them, those words are pure gush. The gentleman in question has been just as mystified as everyone else by the idea of giving dinner parties for the poor, the maimed, the lame, and the blind. But since Jesus ends his remarks with a reference to the "resurrection of the just," this fellow does what so many of us do when confronted with paradox: he takes the first spiritual bus that comes along and gets out of town. In effect he says, "Ah, resurrection! I can't say that I follow your odd little ideas about dining with cripples, but I do agree with what you say about heaven. It's so comforting to hear that everything's going to work out perfectly in the end."

Jesus, in other words, finds himself confronted with a lazy mind. He has said almost nothing about "the end," yet his hearer fastens on it as if he'd talked of nothing else. So Jesus does what he so often does with lazy minds: he applies a rude shock. He launches straight into a story that bumps his hearers off the bus bound for the heavenly suburbs and deposits them back in the seediest part of town.

It's tempting, of course, to take the parable of the Great Banquet as a mere recasting in story form of what Jesus already said discursively at the Pharisee's table. But it is more than that. It begins with a much stronger condemnation of "living" than the actual dinner party did. Earlier in the evening, when Jesus saw the guests vying for the best seats, he gave them a little lecture (appealing to enlightened self-interest) about how their efforts at being winners could very well spoil their enjoyment of the party. But now, in the parable, he portrays the pursuit of a sensible, successful life as something that will keep them—and us—out of the party altogether.

That is the first point about the beginning of the Great Banquet (Luke 14:16): all the excuses given by the first-invited guests are sensible, legitimate excuses. Going to inspect a newly purchased field is as respectable a thing to do with your life as flying out to the coast to discuss the screenplay for a TV special: one is as good a reason as the other why you can't have lunch in New York on Wednesday. And the same is true of test-driving your new fleet of pickup trucks or honeymooning with your latest wife: no host in his right mind would be seriously miffed if you responded to his invitation with such legitimate regrets.

Yet in the parable, the householder not only reacts with anger at their refusals; his anger becomes the moving force behind the party that finally does take place. What are we to make of that? Well, my disposition is to take the vehemence of this party-giver as Jesus' way of dramatizing the futility of "living" as a way of salvation. He is saying that God works only with the lost and the dead—that he has no use for winners. Therefore God will be as furious over legitimate excuses as he would be over phoney ones, since in either case the net result is the same: we keep ourselves out of reach of his gracious action.

There is, of course, a more specific way of interpreting this kind of passage. Whenever Jesus' parables include the note of judgment—of distinguishing who is really "in" and "out"—it is always possible to take them as referring to Jew and Gentile. I find some drawbacks to that, though. The first is that while Jesus was certainly critical of the Jewish establishment of his day, he can hardly have been on the Gentile side of a Jew/Gentile split; he cannot, therefore, legitimately be taken to be as anti-Jewish as this kind of interpretation makes him out. The second is that if you don't ascribe this supposed anti-Jewishness to Jesus himself, you usually end up blaming it on the church. The parables, you say, were probably heavily doctored by the (mostly Gentile) ecclesiastical community of the second century and thus reflected that community's views rather than Jesus'. But to me, that's even less helpful: it drains the authority of Jesus right out of the parables.

My major objection, however, is that I simply do not like bandying about the Jew/Gentile distinction. For one thing, it is so deeply infected by anti-Semitism as to be beyond return to healthy use. Furthermore, it is in the long run irrelevant. Jesus did not save the world as a dead Jew—or as a risen Gentile—he saved it as dead and risen, period. He saved it in our humanity *tout court,* not in any special classification of it. Therefore, whatever his apparent strictures against the Jews—whatever parabolic characters he may have made possible stand-ins for the Jews—he does not intend seriously to suggest that judgment will go against the Jews just because they are Jews, or for that matter, in favor of Gentiles just because they are Gentiles. To me, the fundamental distinctions in Jesus' parables are loser/winner, last/first, dead/alive—not Jew/Gentile. Accordingly, insofar as Jews can legitimately be viewed as objects of judgment in Jesus' parables, it is because, as individuals or groups of individuals, they insist on salvation by winning rather than losing. They are not the enemy: the most that can legitimately be said is that some of them are examples of cooperating with the enemy—which, of course, can be said of every group on earth.

In any case, since the true enemy is "winning" and "living," Jesus proceeds straight to the losers and the dead ducks who form the heart of the parable of the Great Banquet. Here are people who are having the time of their lives—free food, free drinks, free costumes, a Peter Duchin orchestra to dance to—and all on a day when they woke up expecting nothing, if not worse. There was no way they could even have imagined themselves as they are now, the social equals of the winners the host first invited. These are the poor and the handicapped. They don't drive BMWs, they don't own Dior gowns, and they don't tear open their mail in breathless anticipation of yet another gala. These people walk (some of them); they drive, if anything, shopping carts; and they don't get invited anywhere for one simple reason: they are a disgrace to polite, successful society. It's crucial to notice this point, because Jesus is not telling the parable to enforce a moral about being nice to those less fortunate than ourselves. We already knew about that obligation. Rather, he is telling the parable to stand all known values on their heads: hence this bizarre story in which a well-known socialite throws a party for people he found sitting in doorways drinking muscatel out of brown paper bags.

Do you see? The point is that none of the people who had a right to be at a proper party came, and that all the people who came had no right whatsoever to be there. Which means, therefore, that the one thing that has nothing to do with anything is rights. This parable says that we are going to be dealt with in spite of our deservings, not according to them. Grace as portrayed here works only on the untouchable, the unpardonable, and the unacceptable. It works, in short, by raising the dead, not by rewarding the living.

And it works that way because it has no reason outside itself for working at all. That, I take it, is the point of the *two* frenzied searches for extra guests (one into the "streets and lanes" and one into the "highways and hedges"), on which the servant in the parable was sent. They establish that the reason for dragging the refuse of humanity into the party is not pity for its plight or admiration for its lowliness but simply the fact that this idiot of a host has decided he has to have a full house. Grace, accordingly, is not depicted here as a response; above all, it is not depicted as a fair response, or an equitable response, or a proportionate response. Rather it is shown as a crazy initiative, a radical discontinuity—because God has decided, apparently, that history cannot be salvaged even by its best continuities. The world is by now so firmly set on the wrong course—so certain, late or soon, to run headlong into disaster—that God will have no truck with responding to anything inherently its own, whether good or evil. The ship of fools is doomed: if its villains do not wreck it, its heroes will. Therefore there is no point in any continuance, whether of punishment of the wicked or reward of the righteous—no point, that is, in further attempts to redeem the world by relevancy. And therefore in the parable, Jesus has the host make no relevant response at all to the shipwreck of his party; he has him, instead, throw a shipwreck of a party.

In other words, just as the only constant factor in the whole story is the host's monomaniacal determination that his house be full (a determination, please note, that leads him into the curious folly of trying to get even with his first guests by jury-rigging a party they wouldn't be caught dead at anyway), so also the only constant factor in the history of salvation is God's equally monomaniacal commitment to grace. It is precisely that commitment that leads him into the corresponding weakness and foolishness of insisting that being caught dead is the only ticket to the Supper of the Lamb.

Indeed, it seems to me that it is just this foolishness and weakness of God—and the consequently high price of death-resurrection it puts on the otherwise free party—that leads Luke to introduce Jesus' words about the cost of discipleship (Luke 14:25-35; Aland nos. 217-218) immediately after the parable of the Great Banquet. For in this passage, Jesus gathers up all the threads of his teaching about losing and death as the way of salvation. He tells the crowds that if anyone comes to him and does not hate father, mother, wife, children . . . even his own life, he cannot be his disciple. He talks about the necessity of bearing the cross. And then he gives them three short parables to drive home the reality of what he is saying. To convince them he is not just a guru mouthing spiritual truths but a dangerous and expensive operator inviting them into his own dangerous and costly operation, he first tells the parable of the Tower ("Who in his right mind starts a building project without first toting up the cost?"). Next, he adduces the parable of the King Going to War ("If your army is only half the size of your enemy's, you negotiate for peace before he gets to your borders"). Finally, to underscore his meaning, he says plainly (Luke 14:33), "Therefore whoever of you does not renounce his entire substance [hypárchousin: possessions, goods] cannot be my disciple."

Jesus, in other words, gives them the hard sell. "Listen," he says.

"I don't want to waste your time here. What I'm laying out for you is not only the best offer of salvation you've ever seen; it's the only one that will actually work when you get it home. This is the real thing, not some $27.00 fake Rolex Oyster you can pick up on the sidewalk in New York. But unfortunately, even with my spectacularly low overhead, it'll still cost you a bundle. How much? Well, J. P. Morgan said, 'If you have to ask, you can't afford it.' But that was about a yacht, which you could get along without; what I'm selling, you really need. So I say, 'You better ask, because you don't want to be handed the bill on one of your tightwad days and find yourself looking around for a cheaper outfit to deal with.' How much does it cost then? Everything you've got. The works. The whole farm. With no pocket money left over. There are no pockets in a shroud."

Jesus' point, however, is not simply that discipleship in the way of death-resurrection is expensive; more important, it's that it is liberating once the price is paid. For the very next thing he says is the parable of Salt ("Salt is wonderful; but if salt has become insipid how can you make it salty again?"). I have already dealt with other aspects of this parable above in chapter four; here I want simply to underscore its note of liberation. Think about what Jesus is actually saying. On the one hand, it is terrifying and unreasonable: in order to gain salvation, life, and reconciliation, you have to lose every amenity, every relationship, every last scrap of the good life you might have. In short, you have to be dead. On the other hand, the deal is a bargain to end all bargains: sooner or later, you're going to have to lose all those things anyway—willy-nilly, the death that is your wherewithal for buying a new world is already in the bank.

What has that to do with salt? Just this: the saltiness of Jesus' disciples—the taste, zip, and zing that the church at its best can give to the world—derives precisely from our recognition that the Good News is one huge, inside joke. Because it really is a divine comedy. Sure, the price of salvation is high. And sure, you should sit down and count the cost. But do you see what you come up with when you get done counting? You come up with the absolute certainty that *everything you've got* turns out to be exactly the right amount to cut you in on the deal: you have one (1) life, and the price is one (1) life. Even more hilarious than that, you would have to shell out everything anyway, even to get nothing for it. And funniest of all, even if you shell out only because you have to, your total loss will still get you one (1) ticket to the final party. It's exactly like the Great Banquet, in fact: all you have to be is a certified loser and God will send his servant Jesus to positively drag you into his house. And that's the saltiness of the joke: salvation (root: *sal,* which is *salt*) really is free—inconvenient, but free. Which is exactly what salt is: not worth buying for its own sake, but dirt cheap considering the way it perks up everything else.

The only sad thing is that so often the church looks as if it never heard the joke. Either it's afraid to talk about losing and blathers on instead about salvation through moral success, intellectual competence, and spiritual triumph; or if it does finally get around to telling people that death-resurrection is the name of the game, it puts on a long face and acts as if the whole deal is a crying shame. But the Gospel is not a tragedy; it's precisely a hilariously salty story—so flavorful it's in positively bad taste—in which schoolteachers, crane operators, models, bag ladies, arbitrageurs, tennis pros, drug addicts, bankers, lawyers, lechers, and pimps all get away with murder just by dropping dead.

Salvation offerred on any other basis is bad news, not Gospel. We are raised, reconciled, and restored not because we are thrifty, brave, clean, and reverent but because we are dead and our life is hid with Christ in God—because, that is, Jesus has this absolute *thing* about raising the dead. In the Gospels, he never meets a corpse that doesn't sit up right on the spot. "I, if I be lifted up, will draw *all* to me." And if the church can't remember that Good News, then like unsalty salt, it isn't fit to be put anywhere—not on the land, not even on the dunghill; it should simply be thrown as far away as possible. Which, when you think of it, is pretty much what the world has done with the church in the late twentieth century. Maybe the children of this world really are wiser in their generation than the dim-bulb children of light who can't recognize a joke when they hear one.

In any case, all these elaborate appetizers from chapters 14 and 15 having been served up, Luke now brings on the main course, the parable of the Prodigal Son (Luke 15:11-32). He prefaces it, of course (in 15:1-10), with the parables of the Lost Sheep and the Lost Coin, but since I have dealt with those in chapter four above, I shall underline only one thing in them here: they, too, are about a party. Each ends with a celebration, a calling together of friends and neighbors—a rude interruption, mind you, of whatever laundering, housekeeping, bookkeeping, or gardening they may have thought constituted their lives—for a whole afternoon of wine, roses, and laughs. And why? Because by the hilarious constitution of the universe—by the extension of the salty joke into the ultimate shaggy dog story—it turns out that what makes history come out in triumph is some dumb sheep that couldn't find his way home.

But then, to make both the hilariousness and the tastelessness of the joke abundantly clear, Jesus moves on to the parable of the Prodigal Son—and to the biggest, tackiest party yet thrown. George Balanchine was a great choreographer; but if you want to see, in one dramatic presentation, a roundup of all the godawful things that have ever been done with this parable, take a good look at his *The Prodigal Son* next time you have a chance. The father is a forbidding terror; the son comes groveling home; and forgiveness comes only after Baryshnikov has danced his way through enough *tsouris* to keep the entire population of New York depressed for a year. So let me simply expound the story itself, making no effort to hide my enthusiasm for what I think it really says.

The parable is an absolute festival of death, and the first death occurs right at the beginning of the story: the father, in effect, commits suicide. It took me years to notice this fact, but once you see it, it's as plain as the nose on an elephant. The younger son comes to his father and says, "Give me the portion of goods that falleth to me" (I quote from the KJV for heightened contrast). In other words, he tells his father to put his will into effect, to drop legally dead right on the spot. Obligingly enough, the father does just that: he gives the younger son his portion in cash, and to the elder brother, presumably, he gives the farm. Thus, just two sentences into the parable, Jesus has set up the following dynamics: he has given the first son a fat living; he has made the brother, for all the purposes of the parable yet to come, the head of the household; and he has put the real paterfamilias out of business altogether.

Next, of course, Jesus tells us that the younger son went to a far country where his rich boy's life turned rapidly into a lost cause—where he "wasted his substance with riotous living." We are free, naturally, to supply any specific forms of riotousness that appeal to us: boys or booze, girls or drugs, or gambling casinos at $10,000 a night. But whatever the details, the denouement of this part of the story is that the prodigal finally wakes up dead. Reduced to the indignity of slopping hogs for a local farmer, he comes to himself one dismal morning and realizes that whatever life he had is over. (One note about the words for "life" in this parable. The "living" the father divided was *ton bíon,* one of the Greek words for "life." The "goods" that the son requested, and that he wasted intemperately, were *tēn ousían,* which is the Greek for "substance" or "being." In any case, what the father gave away and what the son wasted was not just some stuff that belonged to them; it was their whole existence, their very being, their lives.)

Having thus introduced death into the parable a second time, Jesus proceeds to have the prodigal come face to face with it. He sits him down next to the hog trough and has him look at his life and find . . . nothing. "How many hired servants of my father's," he says, "have bread enough and to spare, and I perish with hunger." And so, in desperation over his own inarguable death—over the end of everything that could possibly be called a life—he formulates the first version of his confession: "I will arise and go to my father, and will say unto him, Father, I have sinned against heaven, and before thee, and am no more worthy to be called thy son: *make me as one of thy hired servants.*"

I have italicized the words at the end of this confession because they show that while the boy may have come face to face with death, he is still far from being able to admit he is in fact already dead. He may understand that he has died as a son—that he has, by his prodigality, lost all claim to his former status as his father's loyal child. But what he does not yet see is that, as far as his relationship with his father is concerned, his lost sonship is the only life he had: there is no way now for him to be anything but a dead son. And because he does not grasp that fact, he formulates a bright new plan of his own for faking out a quasi-life for himself: a life as a hired hand. In short, precisely because he cannot admit he is utterly out of business, he puts himself back in the one business that never ceases to amuse and console the lifeless, namely, the bookkeeping business. He strikes a trial balance, using figures he just fudged in, and prepares himself a trumped-up spreadsheet: sonship he may not be able to claim, but hired-handship . . . ah, there's a possibility. Maybe the old man will be senile enough to make a deal.

So in one sense, the second death in the parable—the death of the prodigal—occurs in the far country. But in the most important sense, in the sense in which he admits it to himself, it does not occur until he comes home. Watch closely, therefore, the details that Jesus now unfolds. "And he arose, and came to his father. But when he was yet a great way off, his father saw him, and had compassion, and ran, and fell on his neck, and kissed him."

Time for a major pause. All the fearsome histrionics Balanchine assigns the father notwithstanding, this is the moment of grace. But to give Balanchine a little credit, it is, like all the moments of a grace that works by raising the dead, a moment of judgment as well—an uttering of the irrevocable sentence of death before resurrection. From the father's point of view, of course, Balanchine is just plain wrong. The father simply sees this corpse of a son coming down the road and, because raising dead sons to life and throwing fabulous parties for them is his favorite way of spending an afternoon, he proceeds straight to hugs, kisses, and resurrection. But from the son's point of view, Balanchine is onto something. In the clarity of his resurrection, the boy suddenly sees that he is a dead son, that he will always be a dead son, and that he cannot, by any efforts of his own or even by any gift of his father's, become a live anything else. And he understands too that if now, in this embrace, he is a dead son who is alive again, it is all because his father was himself willing to be dead in order to raise him up.

And so he makes his confession for the second time: "Father, I have sinned against heaven, and in thy sight, and am no more worthy to be called thy son." Period. Full stop. No hired-hand nonsense at all. End of the subject insofar as the subject lies in his hands.

Time for a pause within the pause. What this parable is saying first of all is that, as far as Jesus is concerned, repentance involves not the admission of guilt or the acknowledgement of fault but the confession of death. Let me quote from myself in *Between Noon and Three:*

> Confession is not a medicine leading to recovery. If we could recover—if we could say that beginning tomorrow or the week after next we would be well again—why then, all we would need to do would be apologize, not confess. We could simply say that we were sorry about the recent unpleasantness, but that, thank

God and the resilience of our better instincts, it is all over now. And we could confidently expect that no one but a real nasty would say us nay.

But we never recover. We die. And if we live again, it is not because the old parts of our life are jiggled back into line, but because, without waiting for realignment, some wholly other life takes up residence in our death. Grace does not do things tit-for-tat; it acts finally and fully from the start. (*Between Noon and Three* [San Francisco: Harper & Row, 1982], p. 77)

And that brings us to the second thing this parable is saying: as far as Jesus is concerned, all real confession—all confession that is not just a fudging of our tattered books but a plain admission that our books are not worth even a damn—is *subsequent to forgiveness*. Only when, like the prodigal, we are finally confronted with the unqualified gift of someone who died, in advance, to forgive us no matter what, can we see that confession has nothing to do with getting ourselves forgiven. Confession is not a transaction, not a negotiation in order to secure forgiveness; it is the after-the-last gasp of a corpse that finally can afford to admit it's dead and accept resurrection. Forgiveness surrounds us, beats upon us all our lives; we confess only to wake ourselves up to what we already have.

Every confession a Christian makes bears witness to this, because every confession, public or private, and every absolution, specific or general, is made and given subsequent to the one baptism we receive for the forgiveness of sins. We are forgiven in baptism not only for the sins committed before baptism but for a whole lifetime of sins yet to come. We are forgiven before, during, and after our sins. We are forgiven before, during, and after our confession of them. And we are forgiven for one reason only: because Jesus died for our sins and rose for our justification. The sheer brilliance of the retention of infant baptism by a large portion of the church catholic is manifest most of all in the fact that babies can do absolutely nothing to earn, accept, or believe in forgiveness; the church, in baptizing them, simply declares that they have it. We are not forgiven, therefore, because we made ourselves forgivable or even because we had faith; we are forgiven solely because there is a Forgiver. And our one baptism for the forgiveness of sins remains the lifelong sacrament, the premier sign of that fact. No subsequent forgiveness—no eucharist, no confession—is ever anything more than an additional sign of what baptism sacramentalizes. Nothing new is ever done, either by us or by God, to achieve anything. It was all done, once and for all, by the Lamb slain from the foundation of the world—by the one God in the Person of the Word incarnate in Jesus. We may be unable, as the prodigal was, to believe it until we finally see it; but the God who does it, like the father who forgave the prodigal, never once had anything else in mind.

All of which takes us straight out of the pause mode and into the party. The father puts no intermediate steps between forgiveness and celebration. There is none of that, "Well, Arthur, you're forgiven; but let's have some good behavior now to make the deal stick"—none of that ungracious talk by which we make the house of forgiveness into a penitentiary. Instead, he turns to his servants and, bent on nothing but the party that life in his house was always meant to be, he commands the festivities to begin: "Bring forth the best robe, and put it on him; and put a ring on his hand, and shoes on his feet: and bring hither the fatted calf, and kill it; and let us eat, and be merry; for this my son was dead, and is alive again; he was lost, and is found."

And there is the third and, if you will, the crucial death in the story: the killing of the fatted calf. Indeed, as far as I am concerned, the fatted calf is actually the Christ-figure in this parable. Consider. What does a fatted calf do? It stands around in its stall with one purpose in life: to drop dead at a moment's notice in order that people can have a party. If that doesn't sound like the Lamb slain from the foundation of the world—who dies in Jesus and in all our deaths and who comes finally to the Supper of the Lamb as the pièce de resistance of his own wedding party—I don't know what does. The fatted calf proclaims that the party is what the father's house is all about, just as Jesus the dead and risen Bridegroom proclaims that an eternal bash is what the universe is all about. Creation is not ultimately about religion, or spirituality, or morality, or reconciliation, or any other solemn subject; it's about God having a good time and just itching to share it. The solemn subjects—all the weird little bells, whistles, and exploding snappers we pay so much attention to—are there only because we are a bunch of dummies who have to be startled into having a good time. If ever once we woke up to the fact that God finally cares only about the party, then the solemn subjects would creep away like pussycats ("Thank God! I thought they'd never leave!") and the truly serious subjects would be brought on: robes, rings, shoes, wines, gold, crystal, and precious stones ("Finally! A little class in the act!").

So now, if we were to sum up the parable thus far, it would be nothing but hilariously good news: the father, the prodigal, and the fatted calf are all dead; they are all three risen (the calf, admittedly, as a veal roast—but then, you can't have everything); and everybody is having a ball. As Jesus put it succinctly: "They began to be merry."

But then comes on (*solemn music:* enter here, in grand procession, the Departments of Ethics and Moral Theology, the Faculty of the School of Religion, the Deans and Trustees of the Law and Business Schools, and the Representatives of the Bursar's Office) the only live character in the parable, the Elder Brother. Mr. Respectability. Herr Buchhalter. Monsieur Comptabilité. The man with volumes and volumes of the records he has kept on himself and everyone else. "And as he came and drew nigh to the house, he heard musick and dancing."

He makes a stagey *contrapposto:* nostrils flared, eyes closed, back of right hand placed against his forehead. He gasps: Music! Dancing! Levity! Expense! And on a working day, yet! "And he called one of the servants, and asked him what these things meant." He is not happy: Why this frivolity? What about the shipments that our customers wanted yesterday? Who's minding the store? "And he [the servant] said unto him, Thy brother is come; and thy father hath killed the fatted calf, because he hath received him safe and sound." He rants: The fatted calf! Doesn't the old fool know I've been saving that for next week's sales promotion when we show our new line of turnips? How am I supposed to run a business when he blows the entertainment budget on that loser of a son? "And he was angry, and would not go in." Finally, therefore, he makes a proclamation: I will not dignify this waste with my presence! Someone has to exercise a little responsibility around here! And Jesus, willing to oblige him with an important audience for all this grousing, sends him one: "Therefore came his father out, and intreated him."

It is easy to stray from the main thrust of the parable at this point. The temptation—since the father has been grace personified to the prodigal—is to read his reply to the elder brother's next words as more of the same tender concern. But since grace works only on the dead, that is a false start. This boy's precise problem is that he refuses to be dead, that he is frantically trying to hold what passes for his life in some kind of gimcrack order. Therefore, since grace cannot possibly work on him, the only proper way to read his father's reply is as judgment—as the brandishing before him of the free saving grace of resurrection from the dead, and the condemnation of all his laborious attempts at living. Watch.

"And he answering said to his father, Lo, these many years do I serve thee, neither transgressed I at any time thy commandment: and yet thou never gavest me a kid, that I might make merry with my friends: But as soon as this thy son was come, which hath devoured thy living with harlots, thou hast killed for him the fatted calf." All of which is pure, unsauced, self-serving tripe. Take *"thy living,"* for example: it wasn't the father's living *(bíon)* any more, because the father died to all that life at the beginning of the parable. Or, take *"wasted"*: while it was indeed wasted, it was probably, on balance, less of a waste than the elder brother's boring life of turnip-counting. Or take *"with harlots"*: as for its having been spent on steamy one-night stands with torrid bar pickups . . . well, that may have been the case, but Mr. Upright here probably wasn't getting himself all worked up like this on the basis of hard information about his brother's habits; more likely, he was getting this stuff straight out of his own two-bit sexual fantasies which, with great interest, he made sure he told God about every day. And as for the *"I've* always been a good boy" line, and the "He gets veal but I never even got to eat goat" nonsense. . . . But enough; time to let the father speak in judgment.

"And he said unto him, Son, thou art ever with me, and all that I have is thine."

You little creep! his father says. What do you mean, *my* living? I've been dead since the beginning of this parable! What your brother wasted was his, not mine. And what you've been so smug about *not* wasting has actually been yours all along. Don't bellyache to me. You're in charge here; so cut out the phoney-baloney. If you were really dying for veal, you could have killed the fatted calf for yourself any day of the week. And if you really wanted to be ready to entertain customers at all hours of the day and night, you would have kept a dozen fatted calves on hand, not just a single measly one you have to have a fit over every time it gets cooked. And as far as your brother's sexual behavior is concerned, listen, Mr. Immaculate

Twinkletoes, you've got a lot to learn. I have no idea how much fun he had getting himself laid, drunk, and strung out, but even if it was only marginal, it was probably more than you've had sitting here thinking.

But see? the father continues, you even get me off the track. The only thing that matters is that fun or no fun, your brother finally died to all that and now he's alive again—whereas you, unfortunately, were hardly alive even the first time around. Look. We're all dead here and we're having a terrific time. We're all lost here and we feel right at home. You, on the other hand, are alive and miserable—and worse yet, you're standing out here in the yard as if you were some kind of beggar. Why can't you see? You *own* this place, Morris. And the only reason you're not enjoying it is because you refuse to be dead to your dumb rules about how it should be enjoyed. So do yourself and everybody else a favor: drop dead. Shut up, forget about your stupid life, go inside, and pour yourself a drink.

The classic parable of grace, therefore, turns out by anticipation to be a classic parable of judgment as well. It proclaims clearly that grace operates only by raising the dead: those who think they can make their lives the basis of their acceptance by God need not apply. But it proclaims just as clearly that the judgment finally pronounced will be based only on our acceptance or rejection of our resurrection from the dead. The last judgment will vindicate everybody, for the simple reason that everybody will have passed the only test God has, namely, that they are all dead and risen in Jesus. Nobody will be kicked out for having a rotten life, because nobody there will have any life but the life of Jesus. God will say to everybody, "You were dead and are alive again; you were lost and are found: put on a funny hat and step inside."

If, at that happy point, some dumbell wants to try proving he really isn't dead . . . well, there is a place for such party poopers. God thinks of everything.

CHAPTER FOURTEEN

The Hardest Parable

The Unjust Steward

The parable of the Unjust Steward (Luke 16:1-13; Aland nos. 222-224) may well be the most difficult of all the parables of Jesus. This story, in which a business manager's crooked attempts to feather his bed after having been fired are first held up for admiration and then made the occasion of obviously critical comments, probably spooks more interpreters into more false starts than any other. Let me list just a few of the devices, desperate and otherwise, that suggest themselves to me as I confront the parable's built-in contradictions.

The first, and worst, is to try to make the whole problem go away by maintaining that Jesus never said these words. This approach—even though it is frequently used to get Jesus off the hook of teaching things his commentators find intellectually disreputable—has two fatal flaws. The first is that there is no way of proving Jesus *didn't* say something when the only source we have says he *did*. Aggressive critics, of course, can always claim they base their conclusions not on other sources but on considerations of "form criticism"; but even for them, the Unjust Steward just sits there in the text stubbornly insisting that Jesus told it. The second flaw in this approach, however, is the really devastating one: if Jesus didn't say this, who did? You might possibly get away with assigning an item like his remarks about divorce and fornication to the hand of some second-century ecclesiastical morality maven, but the Unjust Steward? Derivative minds like that cook up only derivative intellectual concoctions, bland and predictable; they do not produce wildly original dishes like this one.

Admittedly, there is a variation on the "Jesus didn't say it" approach that is less silly—and that is, if you will, more or less inevitable with this parable: I call it the "give Jesus credit for the words but blame every other thing you can on somebody else" gambit. In the case of the Unjust Steward, it works nicely to separate the moralism of the epilogue to the parable from the obviously intended immorality of the parable itself. Here is how you put it into effect.

In your mind's eye, you have Luke sit down at his Gospel-writing desk the morning after he has finished the Prodigal Son, and you have him reach for the pack of index cards containing his so far unused notes on the final journey to Jerusalem. He slips the rubber band off, and what does he find? He finds a whole collection of moralistic bits and pieces about fidelity, covetousness, the law, divorce, scandal, forgiveness, faith, duty, and the coming of the kingdom, plus one miracle (the cleansing of the ten lepers) and four parables: the Unjust Steward, the Rich Man and Lazarus, the Unjust Judge, and the Pharisee and the Publican. How is he to hang all this together? Well, maybe the imagery of the big country house he's just used in the Prodigal Son at the end of chapter 15 can be carried over into the beginning of chapter 16 by starting it off with the Crooked Major Domo story. And then, let's see . . . since that material ends with a crack about unrighteous mammon, maybe he can tuck in some of these scraps about money and trustworthiness and stuff. And then . . . terrific! While he's on the subject, the Rich Man-Poor Beggar story will slide in nicely, and. . . .

But you see the point. He was making an author's decision; and as such choices go, he did remarkably well. His only mistake, probably, was hanging onto all those moral bits and pieces until this late in his Gospel. They sound far more like the early Jesus—the wonder-working rabbi of the Sermon on the Mount—than like Jesus on his way to death and resurrection. And as a matter of fact, when Matthew looked at *his* pack of index cards, he decided that Jesus' warning against trying to serve both God and mammon (Luke 16:13) should, in his own Gospel, go precisely into the Sermon on the Mount at chapter 6, verse 24. In other words, there is actually a textual reason for suspecting that at least the last line of the long version of the Unjust Steward does not necessarily belong to the parable as originally told. So just to lay *my* cards face up for you, here is the way I divide the passage: Luke 16:1-8 is the parable of the

Unjust Steward as such; 16:13 is totally extraneous material attracted to this place because of "mammon"; 16:10-12 is possibly extraneous material attracted for the same reason; and 16:9 is the verse that did all the attracting to begin with and therefore the *crux interpretum* of the whole passage. (I am of two minds about whether verse 9 should be considered part of the actual parable. On the one hand, it shouldn't: verse 8 makes a wonderfully crisp, snappy, Jesus-style ending all by itself. On the other hand, there is so little connection between verses 8 and 9 that I sometimes suspect that no one other than Jesus himself would ever have dreamt of putting them back to back. My solution? In months with 31 days, I read the parable as verses 1-8; in months with 30 days, I read it as verses 1-9; on February 29th, I read it as verses 1-13; and for the rest of February, I thank God it really doesn't matter much how *I* read it anyway.)

In any case, it all boils down to the fact that there are basically just two ways of interpreting this parable: you can make the steward out to be a hero or you can make him out to be a villain. Obviously, if you decide to read the parable as verses 1-8, the white-hat interpretation will be your natural choice; but if you read it as verses 1-13, the black hat will seem to fit better. It's worth noting, though, that each interpretation has a price to it. If you make the steward a bad guy, several things don't make sense. In the first place, the heavily moralized parable that that gives you consists ill not only with the preceding parables in Luke but with the entire tone of the final journey to Jerusalem. Jesus has been on a grace trip for seven chapters now: he has been talking lastness, lostness, death, and resurrection, and he has again and again made it clear that the bookkeeping department's heyday is a thing of the past. Why then, at this stage of the game, would he poke in a parable that has none of the above as its main point—that amounts to little more than a surgeon general's warning that "shady dealing is hazardous to your soul's health"? Above all, why on earth would he put into the parable verse 8 ("And the Lord praised the unjust steward because he had acted shrewdly . . .")—a verse which, unless it is taken as pure sarcasm, makes no sense whatsoever if you take the steward as a plain old bounder?

On the other hand, if you make the steward a good guy, verse 8 becomes the principal support for your interpretation—so much so, that you are willing (as I am) to lop off the rest of the passage in order to do justice to its decisiveness. Even at that price, though, the steward-as-hero interpretation seems preferable: it is, as you will see, consonant with the whole thrust of the parables of grace; in particular, it allows the parable to voice once again the theme of forgiveness-by-resurrection-from-the-dead that is the burden of so much of what Jesus has been saying. It even allows you to entertain the most bizarre and fruitful notion of all, namely, that of the unjust steward as Christ-figure. But more of that shortly. Time now to expound the parable in order.

It begins with some nameless informant telling a certain rich man that his steward has been wasting *(diaskorpízōn)* his money *(hypárchonta,* possessions). Score one fascinating point right there for a "grace" rather than a "morality" interpretation of this parable: *diaskorpízein* is the same verb used in the Prodigal Son to describe the boy's "wasting" of his substance in the far country. From Jesus' very choice of words, therefore, we are given a hint of continuity. Next, the master—without any trial or even fair inquiry—simply reads the steward the riot act: "What's this I hear? You're a disgrace! Turn in your books! You're fired!" Score yet another point for continuity: just as with the Prodigal Son, death enters this parable early, and as a pivotal consideration. The son found himself dead in the far country; the steward comes out of his master's office with none of his old life left at all.

But at this point, the parable of the Unjust Steward diverges from the Prodigal Son and begins to look more like an upside-down version of the Unforgiving Servant. Watch. "So the steward said to himself, 'What shall I do now that my master has taken away my managership? I'm not strong enough to work as a laborer. I'm too proud to be a beggar. Aha! I've got it! I'll use my brains and ace out that unforgiving tyrant. So he wants to play letter-of-the-law games, does he? He would like me to turn in my books, eh? Well, I'll do just that—after I've made a few . . . adjustments.'"

What he does, of course, is call in his master's debtors and settle accounts with them at considerable write-offs: he knocks the bill of one of them down by half, the bill of another by a fifth. All of which might produce a number of different results, depending on how you estimate it. On the one hand, it might at one and the same time make him look bad to his master and good to the debtors. If the master ever remembers any of the originally owed amounts he could be so furious over being gypped that the presence of cash in the till would hardly be enough to mollify him. But then, if the debtors thought kindly of the steward's write-offs, they might, as he hoped, "receive him into their houses" after he was officially fired. On the other hand, his sharp dealing could, with even more logic, be read as making him look good to his master and bad to the debtors. For all we know, the master may have been overjoyed to get even fifty cents on the dollar from deadbeats like those. Likewise, for all we know, deadbeats like those could very likely have spotted the steward as no better than themselves and refused to give him office space.

But whichever of those readings or combination of them you decide to go with, the deciding factor remains verse 8: "And the Lord praised the unjust steward, for the children of this age are wiser in their generation than the children of light." Somehow, between verse 2 ("What's this? You're fired!") and verse 8 ("My beamish boy! You're a genius! I never thought I'd see even a nickel from those accounts!"), the master of the steward has turned from an unforgiving bookkeeper to a happy-go-lucky celebrator of any new interest that comes along. And what has happened to him, can, as I have said, be best understood by comparing this parable with that of the Unforgiving Servant.

In that parable, forgiveness starts from the top down: the lord, who is owed ten million dollars by one of his servants, simply drops dead to his own claim and absolves the debt. His intention, of course, is that the servant will take the hint and likewise drop dead to the hundred dollars owed to him by a fellow servant. But as Jesus tells the story, things do not work out that way—the forgiven servant chooses a bookkeeper's life rather than a spendthrift's death and thus short-circuits the working of forgiveness. Still, the point of the parable remains unchanged: grace works only on those it finds dead enough to raise.

Exactly the same point is made in the parable of the Unjust Steward, but by a reversal of the story's device: forgiveness in this parable starts from the bottom up. Here, it is the lord of the steward who starts out unwilling to drop dead to any of his bookkeeping: he will not die to the steward's peculations, and he will not die to the accounts past due that he has never succeeded in collecting. The steward, however, does die; and because he is freed by his death to think things he could not have thought before, he is the one who, from the bottom of the heap, as it were, becomes the agent of life for everybody in the parable. He becomes life from the dead for his lord, because somehow the sight of a loser bringing off a coup like this in the very thick of his losses finally loosens the old boy up: "My God!" the master says. "My whole life has been a joke, and only now I learn to laugh at it!" But the steward is also able to be the resurrection of his lord's debtors because they wouldn't consent to deal with any-one but a crook like themselves: they would never have gone near him if they hadn't been convinced he was dead to all the laws of respectable bookkeeping.

As far as I am concerned, therefore, the unjust steward is noth-ing less than the Christ-figure in this parable, a dead ringer for Jesus himself. First of all, he dies and rises, like Jesus. Second, by his death and resurrection, he raises others, like Jesus. But third and most important of all, the unjust steward is the Christ-figure because he is a crook, like Jesus. The unique contribution of this parable to our understanding of Jesus is its insistence that grace cannot come to the world through respectability. Respectability regards only life, suc-cess, winning; it will have no truck with the grace that works by death and losing—which is the only kind of grace there is.

This parable, therefore, says in story form what Jesus himself said by his life. He was not respectable. He broke the sabbath. He consorted with crooks. And he died as a criminal. Now at last, in the light of this parable, we see *why* he refused to be respectable: he did it to catch a world that respectability could only terrify and condemn. He became sin for us sinners, weak for us weaklings, lost for us losers, and dead for us dead. *Crux muscipulum diaboli,* St. Augustine said: the cross is the devil's mousetrap, baited with Jesus' disreputa-ble death. And it is a mousetrap for us, too. Jesus baits us criminals with his own criminality: as the shabby debtors in the parable were willing to deal only with the crooked steward and not with the upright lord, so we find ourselves drawn by the bait of a Jesus who winks at iniquity and makes friends of sinners—of us crooks, that is—and of all the losers who would never in a million years go near a God who knew what was expected of himself and insisted on what he expected of others.

You don't like that? You think it lowers standards and threatens good order? You bet it does! And if you will cast your mind back, you will recall that is exactly why the forces of righteousness got rid of Jesus. Unfortunately, though, the church has never been able for very long to leave Jesus looking like the attractively crummy character he is: it can hardly resist the temptation to gussy him up into a respectable citizen. Even more unfortunately, it can almost never resist the temptation to gussy itself up into a bunch of supposedly perfect peaches, too good for the riffraff to sink their teeth into. But for all that, Jesus remains the only real peach—too fuzzy on the outside, nowhere near as sweet as we expected on the inside, and with the jawbreaking stone of his death right smack in the middle. And therefore he is the only mediator and advocate the likes of us will ever be able to trust, because like the unjust steward, he is no less a loser than we are—and like the steward, he is the only one who has even a chance of getting the Lord God to give us a kind word.

"And the lord praised the unjust steward because he had dealt shrewdly": *This is my beloved Son, hear him* (Mark 9:7).

"For the children of this world are shrewder in their generation than the children of light": *And the Word became flesh and dwelt among us . . . full of grace and truth* [John 1:14] *. . . and his own people did not receive him* [John 1:11]. *He emptied himself, taking the form of a servant . . . and finding himself merely human, he humbled himself, becoming obedient to death—death on the cross. Therefore God himself exalted him and graced him with a name that is above any other name, so that at the name of Jesus, every knee will bow . . . and every tongue confess that Jesus Christ is Lord, to the glory of God the Father* (Phil. 2:7-11).

Lucky for us we don't have to deal with a *just* steward.

CHAPTER FIFTEEN

Death and Faith

Lazarus and Dives

There are only two other passages
in Luke 16: a short intermezzo containing a diatribe against
the Pharisees that occasions some comments about the law and
about divorce (verses 14-18; Aland nos. 225-227), and the parable
of the Rich Man and the Poor Man (Dives and Lazarus: verses
19-31; Aland no. 228). The parable, as will be seen, slips effortlessly
into the thematic flow of the final journey to Jerusalem; but the
intervening material (more of those moralistic bits and pieces that
Luke delayed inserting into the narrative) needs a bit of nudging to
get it into the stream. Watch.

Luke's reason for putting in the passage about the Pharisees at
this point seems fairly obvious: its opening verse mentions in passing that they were "lovers of money" *(philárgyroi),* and that they
"were making fun" *(exemyktérizon)* of him. After the material about
mammon he had just added to the parable of the Unjust Steward,
these words no doubt struck him as at least marginally consequential, particularly in view of what appears in verse 15. Jesus tells the
Pharisees, "You are the ones who make yourselves look right in
men's sight, but God knows your hearts. For what is exalted among
men is an abomination before God." This last remark returns Luke
neatly to some of the major themes of Jesus' Jerusalem journey:
human respectability as contrasted with the divine disreputability
and successful living as an ineffective substitute for the lastness and
lostness that alone can save. It brings him back, in short, to the
subject of "life" as the chief impediment to the resurrection of the
dead.

Then, because the Pharisees were nothing if not devotees of the law, Luke finds that some of Jesus' words about John the Baptist and the law will fit in at verse 16: "The law and the prophets [the whole previous revelation of God] were in effect up to the time of John; since then, the kingdom of God is proclaimed as good news and everyone enters into it violently." Once again, Luke is on target: it is not success of any kind that saves—not even success in keeping the law; it is only the violent disruption of all success proclaimed by the Gospel of death and resurrection that can lead to true life in the kingdom.

Finally, though, Luke is confronted with two bits of material whose relevance at this point seems vague to say the least. He includes, at verses 17 and 18, the words "It is easier for heaven and earth to pass away than for the smallest detail of law to be done away with. Every one who puts away his wife and marries another commits adultery; and he who marries a woman thus put away also commits adultery." I can, I think, give a fairly simple rationale for the inclusion of verse 17: it is one of those "if you take the sword, you will perish by the sword" utterances. Jesus, after stigmatizing the Pharisees' reliance on successful law-keeping, simply reminds them—as Paul was to do at length in Romans and Galatians—that the law is not the great, smiling friend they think it is. Since its demands remain perpetually holy, just, and good—and since we are none of those things—the law can only condemn those who rely on their keeping of it to save them.

I am less sanguine, however, about verse 18. Frankly, I think the only reason it appears here is that Jesus, for his own reasons, actually said these words at this point in his ministry (Matthew and Mark also include them in roughly the same time period). In the other two synoptics, they come as part of a response to a question about "putting away a wife" proposed to Jesus by Pharisees; hence they do not seem as "off the wall" as they do in Luke. Accordingly, the question becomes: what conceivable rationale did Luke have for thinking they formed a logical sequence to the verses that precede them? Certainly, there is no way of taking them, in their Lukan context, as *ex professo* teaching about matrimony: that would leave them not only off the wall but totally out of the universe of discourse. All I can conclude is that Luke tucked them in as an illustration of one of the things about the law that so easily condemns. Consider. The Pharisees thought that with a little logic-chopping about "putting away" and "bills of divorcement" they could remarry and still be successful lawkeepers. Jesus simply reminds them that the law's dictate about marriage making two people "one flesh" still stands and thus condemns them as failures. Note, however, that in this verse he does not condemn their failure as much as he does their pointless attempts at success. There is a lesson here for the church: if we are serious about proclaiming a grace that works precisely in failure, collapse, and death, we ought to be charier than we are about excluding matrimonial failure, collapse, and death from the ecclesiastical dispensation of grace. Excommunicating divorced persons on the basis of this passage is a mischievous missing of the very point that Luke makes by including it in this unusual place.

As I said, though, the parable of Dives and Lazarus (Luke 16:19-31) needs no arm-twisting to make it consistent with the larger context of Jesus' teaching at this juncture. It adduces not only the themes of death and resurrection but also those of lastness, lostness, leastness, and littleness; and it also adumbrates—as did the parables of the Prodigal Son and the Unjust Steward—the theme of judgment that will be the burden of Jesus' later parables. Specifically, it enshrines all these themes in a telling story about the contrast between rich and poor. Living well may be the world's idea of the best revenge, and it is certainly the human race's commonest criterion for distinguishing the saved from the lost. But in the mystery of the kingdom, it is precisely living badly—being poor and hungry and covered with repulsive sores—that turns out to be the true vehicle of saving grace. Even a minute's consideration will serve to make that clear.

As I have observed a number of times now, if the world could have been saved by successful living, it would have been tidied up long ago. Certainly, the successful livers of this world have always been ready enough to stuff life's losers into the garbage can of history. Their program for turning earth back into Eden has consistently been to shun the sick, to lock the poor in ghettos, to disenfranchise those whose skin was the wrong color, and to exterminate those whose religion was inconvenient. Nor have they been laggard in furthering that program. On the whole, they have been not only zealous but efficient: witness, to name only a handful of instances, the AIDS crisis, the South Bronx, the apartheid policy in South Africa, and the death camps under Hitler.

But for all that, Eden has never returned. The world's woes are beyond repair by the world's successes: there are just too many failures, and they come too thick and fast for any program, however energetic or well-funded. Dives, for all his purple, fine linen and faring sumptuously, dies not one whit less dead than Lazarus. And before he dies, his wealth no more guarantees him health or happiness than it does exemption from death. Therefore when the Gospel is proclaimed, it stays light-years away from reliance on success or on any other exercise of right-handed power. Instead, it relies resolutely on left-handed power—on the power that, in a mystery, works through failure, loss, and death. And so while our history is indeed saved, its salvation is not made manifest in our history in any obvious, right-handed way. In *God's* time—in that *kairós,* that due season, that *high time* in which the Incarnate Word brings in the kingdom in a mystery—all our times are indeed reconciled and restored *now.* But in *our* time—in the *chrónos,* the sequential order of earthly events, the *low time* of days, years, centuries, and millennia—the shipwreck of history drags on unchanged and unchangeable *now.* And the only bridge between the *now* in which our times are triumphantly in his hand and the *now* in which they are so disastrously in our own is *faith.* The accomplished reconciliation can only be believed; it cannot be known, felt, or seen—and it cannot, by any efforts of ours, however good or however successful, be rendered visible, tangible, or intelligible. Like the servants in the parable of the Wheat and the Weeds, we can only let both the reconciliation and the wreckage grow together until the harvest—until the judgment in which the resurrection finally displays God's time as victorious over ours and allows history to become the party it always tried but never managed to be.

In a way, I feel like apologizing for coming at Dives and Lazarus backwards like this—for putting the cart of the meaning of the parable before the horse of the parable itself, but let it stand. At least you will know where I'm going as I take up the details of the story.

Jesus begins the parable (which appears only in Luke) without preface or explanation. There was a certain rich man, he says, who had a very good life indeed: handmade suits, custom-tailored shirts, a daily menu not a notch below *Lutéce,* and, presumably, a portfolio to bankroll the whole operation indefinitely. Like Nubar Gulbenkian, the legendary financier, he wore out three women, three horses, and three stockbrokers before noon every day.

But outside the heavily guarded gate of Nubar's chateau (shall we call the unnamed rich man Nubar instead of Dives? Let's—just for fun) there was a certain poor man named Lazarus who was covered with sores and rummaged in the garbage for food. Jesus says the dogs came and licked his sores. Those were no doubt Nubar's childrens' cocker spaniels; Nubar's dobermans probably took delight in forcibly reminding Lazarus of just whose garbage he was rummaging in.

In any case, the poor man died and was carried by the angels to the bosom of Abraham; Nubar, finally worn out himself in spite of Brooks Brothers and French cooking, died and was buried; and the scene, as in so many of the best old jokes, shifts to the hereafter. From hell, where the accommodations are well below his accustomed standards, Nubar sees Abraham and Lazarus enjoying an intimate little chat. And he cries out for Abraham to have pity on him and send Lazarus with a nice, cool Campari and soda to take the curse off the infernal heat. Like the Bourbons, Nubar has learned nothing and forgotten nothing. Send Lazarus, indeed! He still thinks of himself as a winner who by divine right can command lackeys like this beggar to fetch him drinks.

So Abraham carefully explains to him the realities of the situation. One: Nubar had a whole lifetime's worth of good things while Lazarus was up to his eyebrows in misery. Two: just in case he hasn't noticed, things have definitely been reversed; score at the end of this last game of his heretofore winning season: Nubar, zero; Lazarus, one thousand. And three: the rules of the league are such that, far from being able to demand overtime in which to even the score, he isn't even going to be allowed to punt. Between us and you, Abraham tells him, there is a great gulf fixed: it's fourth down and ten million yards to go, Nubar. I don't make the rules here, I just call the plays as I see them. The game is over.

Nubar, however, never once having had to take no for an answer in his whole life—never having been at a loss for some way of making a buck out of even the most unpromising situation—falls back on his winner's instincts. Maybe Abraham will give him at least a brownie point if he does a *mitzvah* and arranges to have Lazarus deliver a singing telegram to his five equally rich brothers warning them about the possible disastrous consequences of their present investment programs. Abraham, though, is unenthusiastic. Having Lazarus schlep all over the Middle East ringing doorbells is just another of Nubar's bossy, "when you care enough, send a lackey" ideas. Besides, why should Abraham interrupt the resurrection tête-à-tête he's having, when none of the brothers will listen to advice anyway? Listen, Nubar, he says. They've already had a whole Bibleful of telegrams; they should get them out of the wastebasket and try reading them.

But Nubar, not to be defeated, comes up with one last, desperate play: if he can't make a commercial buck, he'll make a spiritual one. Speaking of resurrection, he says to Abraham, you folks up there are missing out on a good thing. You send Lazarus to my brothers, and guaranteed, you'll get results. This would not be your ordinary phone-it-in message; this would be in-person-from-the-other-side-of-the-grave service. Believe me, Nubar says, I know what impresses a client.

So Abraham takes a deep breath and delivers the punch line of the parable. Look, Nubar, he says. I'm going to tell you something. When we talk resurrection up here, we're not talking about some dumb, corpse-revival scheme in which the dead get up and go back to the same old life they had before. We're talking about a whole new order that actually works through death, loss, and failure. And in order to give people even a hint of that, the one thing we don't do is send back revived corpses. The way we've got it worked out, even when the incarnate Word himself gets raised from the dead, he only hangs around for forty days: then . . . pffft! Because you know what would happen if we left him there? They'd never in a million years get the idea that the resurrection was a new order they could get in touch with only by faith—only by *trusting* it; instead, they'd figure it was just one more funny wrinkle in the grimy face of history and they'd try to sell it as something that was merely interesting—as *news,* for crying out loud! If we left the risen Word on earth, they'd right away get him on *Good Morning America* and *Sixty Minutes,* then on *Carson* and *Donahue*—and then, for all I know, on *Hollywood Squares.* After that, probably, it would be *Jesus, The Movie,* followed by *Jesus, I through VI.* They're dumb, Nubar. Dumb, dumb, dumb. Just like you. So this is how it stands. Your brothers have Moses and the prophets, and they'll also get the risen and ascended Word.

That's enough for anybody who's willing to *believe*. But for people who are hanging around, waiting to be *convinced*. . . Listen, Nubar; I'm sorry, but we've got a bad connection here. Must be the great gulf. I'm hanging up.

But enough. Death-resurrection stands forth as clearly in this parable as it does in any of the others. And the successful life is just as roundly condemned. Lazarus starts out as a loser, plays out his allotted hand, and then, in one stunning throw, wins the game with the last trump of an accepted death. Dives starts out as a winner, but because he never accepts death (witness his incessant *handeling* with Abraham, his cooking up of one life-saving deal after another), he loses, hands down. Jesus is anticipating the parable of the Pharisee and the Publican here. In that story, too, both main characters are dead: the difference between them is simply that while the publican accepts his death and is justified, the Pharisee rejects his and is condemned.

And the ending of the parable of Dives and Lazarus makes this point once and for all: "If they will not hear Moses and the prophets, neither will they be persuaded, though one rose from the dead." For those convinced that living is the instrument of salvation, death is such an unacceptable device that they will not be convinced, even by resurrection. From the point of view of those who object to the left-handedness of the Gospel, you see, Jesus' mistake was not his rising in an insufficiently clear way and then sailing off into the clouds. That, if anything, was only a tactical error. His great, strategic mis-calculation was dying in the first place: after such a grievous capitulation to lastness and loss, no self-respecting winner could even think of doing business with him.

It is not, of course, that we are to run out and actively seek a miserable life like Lazarus's. Contrary to the misreading of the spir-itual advice of earlier centuries (for example, the go-hunt-for-trou-ble interpretation of Donne's, "Be covetous of crosses, let none fall"), we are not to go searching for loathesome diseases and rotten breaks. Life in this vale of tears will provide an ungenteel sufficiency of such things (witness Keble's, "The trivial round, the common task/ Will furnish all we ought to ask"). The truth, rather, is that the crosses that will inexorably come—and the death that will inevitably result from them—are, if accepted, all we need. For Jesus came to raise the dead. He did not come to reward the rewardable, improve the improvable, or correct the correctible; he came simply to be the resurrection and the life of those who will take their stand on a death he can use instead of on a life he cannot.

And so Lazarus is the Christ-figure in this parable. Like Jesus, he lives out of death. For those willing to trust the left-handed working of God already disclosed in the law and the prophets (it is the passion of Israel, not its success, that is the *leitmotiv* of Scripture), the mere assertion of Lazarus's triumph, like the mere proclamation of Jesus' resurrection, is all the evidence they are going to get. For those who are unwilling to make a decision to trust such a proposition, however, nothing will be enough to persuade them. But then, that was obvious all along: because like Dives, they will always be in the untenable position of insisting on *something* in a universe where it is precisely out of *nothing* (at the end as well as at the beginning) that God brings all things into life and being.

Death, you see, is absolutely all of the resurrection we can now know. The rest is faith.

CHAPTER SIXTEEN

The Scandal of the Gospel

The Returning Servant, the Ten Lepers, and the Vultures

In chapter 17 of his Gospel (Al-
and nos. 229-235), Luke continues stitching in the remaining bits
of material—many of them parabolic in nature, if not actually parables in their own right—that he has marked for inclusion in Jesus'
final journey to Jerusalem. At first glance, it looks like mere patch-
work, one small pericope following another with no particular
design; but on closer examination, I find it to be as consistent a
tissue of lastness, littleness, and death as any of the preceding chapters.

He begins (Luke 17:1-2) with Jesus' saying that "It is inevitable
that *skándala* will come, but woe to the one by whom they come. It
would be better for him if a millstone were hung around his neck
and he were cast into the sea than that he should *skandalísę* one of
these little ones." Obviously, the crucial word here is *skándala:* scan-
dals, causes of offense, temptations to sin, things that make people
fall into sin. I have deliberately left it untranslated in order to allow
the context to dictate its meaning.

In many of the root word's uses in the New Testament, *skándalon* (and its verb form, *skandalízein*) refers simply to something
that occasions sin or temptation. Look, for example, at Matt. 13:41
(in Jesus' interpretation of the parable of the Wheat and the Weeds),
where it is said that "the Son of man will send his angels . . . and they
will gather out of his kingdom all the *skándala,* along with those
who do lawless things." See also Matt. 16:23 (right after Peter's
confession and Jesus' first prediction of his death and resurrection),
where Jesus replies to Peter's refusal to listen to this death-talk by
saying "Get behind me, Satan; you are a *skándalon* to me." On other

occasions, however, the word is used to refer to what Paul, in Gal. 5:11, calls "the *skándalon* of the cross," namely, the weakness, foolishness, and general offensiveness of the left-handed method of salvation at work in the death and resurrection of Jesus. This usage also occurs not only in Rom. 9:33, "I will set in Zion a stone of stumbling and a rock of *skandálou*" (he is referring to the dead and risen Christ), but also in Rom. 11:9, "Let their table [Israel, that is, in their rejection of the dying/rising Messiah] be to them . . . a snare and a *skándalon*," as well as in 1 Cor. 1:22-23, "the Jews seek a sign and the Greeks, wisdom; but we preach Christ crucified, to the Jews a *skándalon* and to the Greeks, foolishness."

The question comes therefore: in which of these two senses—as a general *occasion of stumbling* or as the specific *offensiveness of Jesus' left-handed salvation*—is the word *skándalon* used in this passage and in its parallels at Matt. 18:6 and Mark 9:42? To my mind, the answer has to be the latter sense. I am persuaded of that by the inclusion, in all three places, of the concluding reference to *scandalizing* "one of these little ones." Once again, we are back at the saving littleness—the lostness and the lastness that Jesus continually contrasts to the pointless pursuit of greatness and the vain effort to win that characterizes the world's efforts to save itself. Taken in context, therefore, what this passage says is that the scandal of the cross is inescapable: it would be better for someone to meet a violent end than to be guilty of making one of these "little ones"—one, that is, who already has a grip on the operative device of grace—think that his littleness is itself a *skándalon*, an occasion of failure to be avoided rather than embraced.

That much established, the rest of the section (Luke 17:3-10) makes eminently consistent sense. Verses 3 and 4, about forgiving a repentant brother even if he sins against you seven times a day (a variant on the preface to the parable of the Unforgiving Servant in Matt. 18), turn out to be about the same subject as that parable, namely, the truth that only those willing to lose can ever really win: if you insist on being a success and on admitting only certifiable moral successes into your circle of friends, you are simply going to be out of luck as far as the process of salvation is concerned.

Verses 5 and 6 likewise become consequential. The apostles say to Jesus, "Increase our faith." They sense, apparently, that he is inviting them yet again to adopt an outlook on life that is contrary to all their right-handed notions of how life ought to be lived. They hear, in these remarks about saving littleness and unlimited, life-laying-down forgiveness, a command to act contrary to all their normal instincts. And they conclude, quite naturally, that they haven't got the spiritual resources to sustain such a program. Jesus' reply, though, is a shocker. In spite of the fact that his words ("If you had faith as big as a mustard seed, you could say to this mulberry tree, 'Pull yourself up by the roots and plant yourself in the sea,' and it would obey you") have been given all kinds of "make-a-greater-spiritual-effort" interpretations, they seem on balance to mean just the opposite. The apostles ask for more faith; Jesus tells them that if they had even less than they have now (faith "like a mustard seed" has got to be very little faith) the preposterous and the impossible would seem as easy as pie and as sensible as shoes.

He tells them, in other words, that even when it comes to faith, they don't have to be winners. One of the most iniquitous ways of expounding the Gospel is to say that while we will no doubt have to put up with physical or financial failure for Jesus' sake, we are none-theless entitled to expect moral and spiritual success. But that is itself a snare and a *skándalon*. It says that we are only half fallen—that even though the ratty old cocoon of our physical being may fail us, there is hidden within it a spiritual butterfly of a soul that is capable of beauty, competence, and success. And it usually goes on to add that what we need to actualize all that gorgeousness is not a redeemer who dies—not a paradoxical savior who expects us too, physically *and* spiritually, body *and* soul, to die with him—but only a guide, a teacher, a guru, a dispenser of some slick, esoteric *gnôsis* who will, with no death at all, enable us to realize our potential as spiritual beings.

Don't get me wrong. I am not against saying that the realization of our spiritual potential is one of the promises of Christ; I just want to add two footnotes to what spiritual fast-talkers usually have to say on the subject. The first is that the Gospel holds up before us the promise of a realization of our physical potential as well: as we maintain in the creed, we believe in the resurrection of the *body*—of the *flesh*. The second is that whether we hope for physical *or* spiritual perfection, the Gospel promises us neither except by death and resurrection. Golgotha and the empty tomb are not just some guru's shtick. They are not the incidental stage business of a swami's mock exit into some blue empyrean we all have inside us anyway. They are, in and as themselves, the very sacrament—the real presence—of the unique mystery of salvation. And no man or woman—however burdensomely physical or magnificently spiritual—comes to the Father except by him who died on the cross and rose from the grave.

So but me no spiritual buts. And above all, faith me no faith that needs to be made greater, or purer, or warmer. It is not as if we have a faith meter in our chests, and that our progress toward salvation consists in cranking it up over a lifetime from cold to lukewarm to toasty to red hot. We cannot be saved by our faith reading any more than by our morality reading or our spirituality reading. All of those recipes for self-improvement amount to nothing more than salvation by works; and none of them is any better than the idea that you might be saved by being able to go twenty hours nonstop on a Nautilus machine. If we have anything in our chests, it is not a metaphysical pulse register or an ethical pressure gauge but a simple switch: *on*, for *yes* to Jesus in our death; and *off*, for *no*. The head of steam we work up in throwing the switch, either way, has nothing to do with the case.

As a matter of fact, I am willing to push my interpretation of "faith like a mustard seed" all the way to an absurdity that matches Jesus' absurdity of the mulberry tree jumping into the ocean. Even faith is not the essential thing. Even if your switch is off—even if you say no to Jesus all your life, and forever after as well—you still die; and out of your death, Jesus still raises you. *That* is how the universe works, not by the endless refinement of spiritual gas. "I, if I be lifted up, will draw *all* to myself": he gets every last one of us, willy-nilly. True enough, we will never enjoy the eternal Supper of the Lamb unless we say yes to it: unless we put on the wedding garment of our acceptance of his acceptance of us, we will spend eternity gnashing our teeth in the darkness outside the party. But the party remains unpoopable: the precise hell of hell is that even if we never go back into the wedding reception, his endless, nagging invitation to the celebration will beat forever like hailstones on our thick, self-condemned heads.

I apologize for all that time on faith like a mustard seed—but not very seriously, because of the verses that follow. In Luke 17:7-10, Jesus ties off the threads of this tissue of littleness and leastness with a demi-parable. Just to make sure the apostles understand clearly that they must not turn faith into a work, he sets them a mental exercise. Suppose, he says, one of you has a slave who comes in from twelve hours hard labor in the field. What do you say to him? Have a seat, Mischa, and let me get you some chopped liver and a little chicken soup? You do not! You say, Mischa, rattle those pots and pans and serve me some supper; then you can eat. And do you thank him when he does it? You do not! It was his job. Remember that the next time you want some kind of super faith or expect me to be super happy because you think you've got it. You've got only one job to do and that's to drop dead for me. That's all I need from you, because everything else that needs doing, *I* do. And I'm not going to thank you for what you do, or reward you for what you achieve, because no matter how nifty any of it may be, it's all useless for my purposes—all tainted, like even your faith, with your boring commitment to winning. I'm just going to come to you in your death, and raise you up with my life, and then say, Mischa, c'mon up here with Arthur and Lazarus and all the rest and let's you and me have a ball.

In any case, the next thing that Luke records is Jesus' cleansing of ten lepers (Luke 17:11-19). The time and place of the action are given only loosely: the healing takes place "on the way to Jerusalem" at the outskirts of "a certain village" somewhere "between Samaria and Galilee." Luke puts the story here, I think, because he reads it as an *acted* parable illustrating the same general points that Jesus' spoken parables have been making: it is about losers who, because of their ostracizing affliction, were dead to ordinary social life; and it is about the fact that resurrection from the dead cannot be recognized, let alone be enjoyed, except on the basis of the acceptance of death.

The episode, however, has a number of twists and turns in it. Ten lepers, standing well away from Jesus as they were supposed to, call out, "Jesus, Master, have mercy on us." He looks at them, and then tells them to go and "show themselves to the priests." This is the first twist. Jesus is referring to Lev. 14:2-3—a passage that specifies the ceremonies for the removal of *ritual* defilement from a leper who is already physically clean. In other words, he is telling them—while they are still lepers, still losers, still dead to ordinary life—to act as if they were healed and no longer outcasts. They, however, say nothing; they simply go. Luke leaves it unclear whether they took Jesus seriously and were on their way to the priests, or just went away in confusion over such a bizarre reply to their plea for mercy. Whichever it was, though, "as they went, they were healed."

Nine of them, of course, just kept going. Apparently, they made no connection between Jesus' "spacey" reply and their recovery. This is the second twist in the story; and it's hard to blame them for what they did. From their point of view, Jesus didn't do anything like what they may have had in mind: no touching, no commanding words, not even the simple "I will; be healed" that he used at other times. For them to have concluded that Jesus himself was responsible for their cleansing was no easy matter of putting two and two together: their leprosy was a *two* and their healing, a *four;* but where the other *two* came from was not at all clear.

The tenth leper, though, when he sees that he is healed, comes back loudly praising God and falls at Jesus' feet saying, Thank you, thank you, thank you. "And he," Luke says, "was a Samaritan." Which makes twist number three: this man is a twofold outcast, a double loser, a duck twice dead. But Jesus' reply to him is no less perplexing than anything else in the story so far: he says (to the bystanders, it appears, not to the leper), "Hey, weren't there ten who were healed? Where are the other nine? How come we can't find anybody who came back and thanked God except this foreigner?" Only then, finally, does he speak to the Samaritan himself: "Get up and go," he says; "your faith has saved you."

What are we to make of this? The nine, who presumably had no such faith as the Samaritan, were not one bit less healed than he. What difference is Jesus trying to pinpoint between him and them with this terse, if not gruff, reply? Well, I can think of two ways of coming at it, one more or less doctrinal and the other based on the parable of the Prodigal Son.

The doctrinal approach looks at the lepers as an illustration of the resurrection of the dead: just as *all* the dead (not merely the just, the holy, and the good) are raised by Jesus, so all the lepers (not just the perceptive and thankful) are cleansed. But for the lepers to enjoy, to accept, to celebrate the power of their resurrection from the disease . . . well, that cannot happen until they see themselves not simply as returned to normal life by some inexplicable circumstance but precisely as lepers cleansed by Jesus—that is, as living out of their death by the gift of someone else's life. So too with the resurrection of the dead: it is not the return of corpses to their previous living state; it is an eternally new creation arising out of an equally eternal *death*—just as, if you will, our old, natural existence is a perpetual, moment-by-moment emergence out of an equally perpetual *nothing*.

Which brings me to the approach based on the Prodigal Son. The nine lepers in this story are like the son when he formulates the first version of his confession to his father. Like him—as he sits by the hog trough in the far country—they realize they are dead. But also like him, their idea of resurrection is just a matter of revival, of return to some form of ordinary life. The prodigal makes plans to get himself hired on as a servant; the nine lepers, possibly, propose to go back to the garment district and find work as pressers.

The Samaritan leper, however, is like the prodigal when he makes his confession the second time and leaves off the part about "make me a hired servant." For just as the prodigal suddenly sees—when his father kisses him *before* he confesses—that he can only be a dead son who has been raised to a new life, not a hired hand trying to fake out an old-style life of his own, so the Samaritan realizes that it is by his relationship to Jesus, and by that alone, that he now has a new life out of death as a leper. It is not, you see, that either of them is told to forget about the death out of which he has been raised, or to put it behind him, or to "get on with his life." That was what the nine lepers, and the prodigal in his first self-examination, had in mind—and it is, unfortunately, what far too many Christians think about their risen life in Jesus. But the prodigal's startlingly new life (Party! Party! Party!) is, by the very words of the parable, based squarely and only on his death ("Let us eat and be merry: for this my son was dead and is alive again"). Death, in other words, remains the perpetual reason for the party and the abiding ground of the new creation—for the prodigal, for the Samaritan leper, and for us.

And what a gift that is! It means that contrary to all the cartoons of heaven as a place where we shall sit on clouds wearing bedsheets and flapping irrelevant angel wings—as a place, that is, where none of our real history, and certainly none of the diseases, defeats, derelictions, and deaths of our history can find a home—contrary to all that, *everything* about us goes home, because everything about us, good or evil, dies in our death and rises by his life. The son's prodigality goes home, the Samaritan's leprosy goes home; and so does your lying, my adultery, and Uncle Harry's embezzling. We never have to leave behind a scrap! Nothing, not even the worst thing we ever did, will ever be anything but a glorious scar.

And that *is* a gift, because it means we don't have to deny one smitch of our history. The nine lepers go away with their lives unsaved precisely because their lives as lepers have been put behind them and denied. All those years . . . just *gone*—into unsalvageable oblivion, into irretrievable discontinuity: "Who, me? A leper? You must be kidding, buddy. I'm a pants presser." But the Samaritan goes away with his life saved because, like the prodigal, he has not put his derelict life into the forgettery. At Jesus' feet he sees himself whole: dead *and* risen, an outcast *and* accepted, a leper *and* cleansed. And he sees himself that way because, like the prodigal, he has not hated the light and he has not lived the lie of trying to keep his wretchedness away from the light; rather he has *done the truth* (John 3:21), and *come to the light* with the whole sum of his life, so that it might be clearly seen, in the light of Jesus' resurrection, that everything he ever did, good or bad, *was done in God.*

And just to round out this rhapsody of death and resurrection—of the saving, rather than the trashing, of our history—Luke puts in, as the concluding section of chapter 17, Jesus' longish reply to a short question from the Pharisees. Why this apocalyptic material, and why here? Well, because it follows logically: presumably, the Pharisees have been part of Jesus' audience since at least Luke 16:14; and they have been less than happy with all his mumbo jumbo about the lost, the little, and the dead. "Enough with these paradoxes!" they say. "Let's get this show on a road we can understand. Tell us, Master, in twenty-five words or less: *When will the kingdom of God come?*" (Luke 17:20).

They don't, of course, get what they asked for. Instead, they get still more paradox and mystery. "The kingdom of God," Jesus says, "does not come in such a way as to be seen [*metá paratēréseōs*, with watching]. Nobody's going to say, 'Here it is!' or 'There it is!' Because from what I've been saying, it should be obvious to you that the kingdom of God is *already here in your midst* [*entós hymõn*: among you, or within you]—hidden, that is, in your lostness and death."

Then, turning to the disciples who are going to have to peddle this mystery after he's dead, risen, and ascended, Jesus tries to give them a bit more of a handle on it. "The days are coming," he says, "when you will absolutely ache [*epithymḗsete*, desire strongly] to see one of the days of the Son of man, but there won't be anything to see. You may have an overpowering urge to point to something, anything, that might be a visible proof that I have some more marketable plan than the apparent do-nothing-nowhere-nohow program I've given you to sell; but in fact I have no other plan. And the program I do have will not, *in your time,* give you a shred of evidence other than your faith to offer the world. So everyone else will have a field day running around and shouting, 'Look! *There's* the action of God, right over there in Scranton, PA,' or '*Here's* where the action is, right here on this wonderful TV healing show brought to you live from the diving board of the original pool of Siloam.' But when they start that nonsense, for God's sake don't go running after them or follow their example, because it's not going to be like that at all. Actually, the coming of the Son of man will be more like lightning: sort of everywhere at once, lighting up the whole world—not just Scranton or somebody's swimming pool."

"But first," Jesus says, "the Son of man is going to suffer a lot and be rejected by everybody." You know what it's going to be like? he says to them. It's going to be like it was in the days of Noah. Noah was one of the first to be in on the mystery of death and resurrection, but people paid no attention whatsoever to him. He was a sign that the whole world was going down the drain of death and that God had plans to use that death to save it; but they wouldn't think about anything but their precious little lives, their two-bit plans for the season. They had dinner parties to go to, weddings to plan, swimming pools to get the algae out of. And they went right on doing all that, clear up to the very day that Noah got into the ark and the flood came and destroyed them all. The same thing was true in the days of Lot in Sodom. Everybody just went crazily on, living for all they were worth, until the fire and brimstone came pouring down on them from the sky.

Don't you see? Jesus asks them. The message I'm sending you out to proclaim is that death is safe for those who trust in me; but for those who are committed only to what they call "life" . . . well, they just can't accept that. So when the Son of man is finally revealed—when my hidden working in the deaths of the world is made manifest at the last day—all those folks are going to be very unhappy. Still, since I'm going to raise them all anyway, they'll always have a shot, as long as they're willing to cut out the "life" malarkey and accept death and resurrection. For instance. If somebody's up on the roof replacing shingles and he sees me risen from the dead, he should definitely not go down into the house to get his Visa card and splash on a little cologne. And if somebody's out plowing the south forty, he shouldn't go back to the old homestead and finish his tax return. Remember Lot's wife: when the action was finally out in the open and it was time for her to go with the flow, she decided to have a nostalgia binge and look back at the scene of all her lovely alfresco suppers with the Sodom social set. What did it get her? It got her turned into a pillar of salt, that's what. So keep her in mind: you try to save your life like that and all you'll do is lose it. But if you're willing to go with the action in my death and yours—which is the only action in town—you'll get your life back in spades. But I'll tell you something. It's not going to be easy for people to accept that, and it certainly won't be easy for you to figure out why one person buys it and another doesn't. You'll see two buddies on a hunting trip zipped into the same sleeping bag: one of them will say yes to death and resurrection and one of them will say no. You'll see two women having a nice kaffeeklatsch in a sunny kitchen: one of them will go for the deal, the other will say she has to think about it forever.

But now Jesus makes up for his long answer to a short question with the punch line of the whole chapter. The disciples—just as confused by all this as the Pharisees—come back at him with the very same question. "But *where*, Lord?" they ask. And Jesus says, "Where the corpse is, that's where the vultures will congregate."

Of all the big-help, thank-you-for-nothing answers Jesus ever gave, this one takes the cake. At least it seems to until you see it in the light of my paraphrase of Luke 17:20-36: then it becomes as clear as . . . lightning. Because when you take that whole passage as a rhapsody on death, his words about corpses and vultures say only one thing. Jesus says to them in effect, Don't worry about *where* when it comes to resurrection: you put a dead sheep anywhere, and the vultures will find it. Don't you see what that means? You can put the dead of the world anywhere—some of them even in Scranton—and the Son of man will zero in on every last one. The dead are my *dish*, kiddies. They're where I work. Raising them is what I *do*. The living, unfortunately, I can't do much for; but the nice thing is that even they're not a total loss. Because even they die sooner or later and . . .

well, as I said, wherever the corpses are, this old vulture's going to find them and raise them up.

So skip all the *where* business, Jesus concludes, and forget about the *how* and the *when* part too. All that matters is that you trust me to do the job, and that you get yourselves out there beating the bushes and inviting everybody else to trust me too. It really is all safe, you know: nobody's got anything to lose but a life that's a loser anyway. Where there's death, there's hope.

Death—to say it once again—is absolutely all of the resurrection we can now know. The rest is faith.

CHAPTER SEVENTEEN

God as Anti-hero

The Unjust Judge

The last two parables of grace I shall deal with in this book are Jesus' stories of the Unjust Judge (Luke 18:1-8; Aland no. 236) and the Pharisee and the Publican (Luke 18:9-14; Aland no. 237). For two reasons. First and simplest, Luke 18:14 is the point at which the Aland chronology leaves the Lukan account of the last journey to Jerusalem and switches back to Matthew for the account of Jesus' final ministry in Judea before Palm Sunday. But more important than that, Jesus' gradual shift from the theme of grace to that of judgment has now become pronounced enough to warrant tying off the parables of grace as such.

Admittedly, my choice of these two parables as the place for the final knot is a bit arbitrary: the note of grace will continue to sound for a while after this point, and the theme of judgment has already been introduced before it. Grace, for example—with its operative devices of lastness, lostness, littleness, and death—will still be featured in passages yet to come: in Jesus' blessing of little children (Matt. 19:13-15), in the acted parable of the Rich Young Man (Matt. 19:16-30), in the Laborers in the Vineyard (Matt. 20:1-16), in the acted parable of the Raising of Lazarus (John 11), and in Jesus' third prediction of his passion and death (Matt. 20:17-19). But by the same token, judgment has been an element in his parables since at least chapter 14 of Luke: the Great Banquet, the Prodigal Son, the Unjust Steward, Dives and Lazarus, the acted parable of the Cleansing of the Ten Lepers, and the discourse on the coming of the kingdom—all of which I have already dealt with in chapters twelve through sixteen above—have judgment as a notable subtheme. Between the Aland chronology and the co-presence of the two themes, therefore—not to mention the already considerable length of this volume—I feel reasonably justified in my decision to make an end after just two more parables.

The Unjust Judge, like the Good Samaritan and the Unjust Steward, is another notable example of Jesus' use of an anti-hero. Never having been to a theological seminary, he was blessedly free of the professional theologian's fear of using bad people as illustrations of the goodness of God. There is an old seminarians' joke that stigmatizes this don't-let-God-be-disreputable attitude perfectly: You go to seminary to learn about all the things God couldn't possibly have done, and then you go to church to ask him to do them anyway. In the spirit of that healthy skepticism, I proceed straight to the exposition of the parable itself.

The parable is prefaced with a comment by Luke that Jesus told it as a lesson to people that they ought always to pray and not become discouraged. While this is by no means an unfair or irrelevant hint as to the parable's meaning, I still think that on balance it is a case of Homer nodding. Luke is still using up his last few index cards here; and while his decision to insert the Unjust Judge at this point puts it brilliantly in context (whether you take it as dealing with either grace or judgment), he really should not simply have copied into the text the rather general, early-Jesus-style introduction he originally jotted down for it in his notes.

Be that as it may, the parable itself begins at Luke 18:2: "There was a certain judge *[kritḗs]* in a certain city who neither feared God nor respected public opinion." This is a bold stroke on Jesus' part. He is about to take two subjects that most people find diametrically opposed—the grace business and the judging business—and expound them conjointly. Here is a jurist, a practitioner of the law, whom Jesus will portray as a barefaced agent of grace—and whom he will portray that way precisely because he breaks the rules of his profession and puts himself out of the judging business. All of which, Jesus implies without apology, makes him a perfect stand-in for God. He suggests, in other words, that God is not cowed by the supposed *requisita* and *desiderata* of the God-business any more than he is impressed by the rules that people (especially theologians) have dreamt up for him to follow.

Jesus then continues by saying there was a widow *(chḗra)* in that city who came to the judge asking him to render her a favorable judgment *(ekdíkeson me)* against her adversary. The choice of a widow for the other character in this parable is a stunning device for displaying the antithesis between losing and winning that recurs constantly in the parables of grace. On the one hand, the woman is a twenty-four karat loser: widows, especially in ancient times, were people who had lost not only their husbands but their social standing—they had, in a word, lost their life as they knew it. But this particular widow is also a compulsive winner. Like so many of us who, while we may be poor, still go blithely on rejecting our poverty and trying to fake out some kind of wealth—who are, in the last analysis, just high rollers who happen to be unaccountably and embarassingly broke—she is still committed to making a buck out of her loss. Like the prodigal son when he first formulates his confession, she is dead and she knows it, at least to some degree; but she has not really accepted her death because she still hopes she can ace out the system and get some old-style, if marginal, satisfaction from it.

For a while *(epí chrónon)*, Jesus says, the judge tells her to go fly a kite. Her suit, no doubt, strikes him as having nothing but nuisance value to anyone but herself: he will not have his calendar clogged up with a case that no self-respecting jurist would give even the time of day. (Note here, in passing, the word *chrónos* in the phrase "for a while." I am at least a little tempted to lean on it briefly. *Chrónos,* I take to refer to *our* time: *historical* time, *sequential* time, the *low* time in which we so disastrously try to win by winning. But in the parable, Jesus goes on to say that *afterward [metá taúta]* the judge had a change of heart. I suggest that this *after time* might possibly stand for the *kairós,* the *high time of God* in which alone our time is finally reconciled.)

Then, however, Jesus goes on to give the judge's reasoning for his change of heart. "Even though I don't fear God or respect public opinion," the judge says to himself, "still, simply because this widow is giving me such *tsouris,* I will grant her a favorable judgment—just so she doesn't finally wear me out *[hypōpiázē me]* by her constant showing up in my courtroom." He arrives at his judgment, you see, not on the merits of the case but simply on the basis of his own convenience. He is willing to be perceived as a bad judge just so he can have a little peace of mind.

And what does that say about God? It says that God is willing to be perceived as a bad God—and for no better reason than that he wants to get the problems of a worldful of losing winners off his back. It says he is willing—while they are still mired in their futile pursuit of the spiritual buck, the moral buck, the intellectual buck, the physical buck, or the plain ordinary buck—to just shut up about whatever is wrong with them and get the hassle over with. It says in fact what Paul said in Rom. 5:8: "While we were yet sinners, Christ died for us." It says, in short, that God doesn't even wait for us to accept our losing: he simply goes ahead with his own plans for the season, for the *kairós,* the *high old time* he has in mind for himself. Like the father in the Prodigal Son, he just runs, falls on all our necks—the widow's and yours and mine—and showers us with injudicious kisses simply because he wants to get the wet blankets off his back and let the party begin.

The prodigal, of course, responded positively to the father's ungodly behavior: he left out of his actual confession the silly, life-preserving gesture of asking to be made a hired servant and he frankly accepted his status as a dead son who had been raised. The widow does not seem to have responded so favorably to the judge's gift of grace, but the outcome is the same: the son is justified and she is justified. And the words she uses to ask the judge for a favorable verdict (*ekdíkēson me,* justify me) and the words the judge uses to announce his intention to do precisely that (*ekdikḗsō autḗn,* I will justify her) both contain the root *dik-*. This root enters into a whole string of major New Testament words: *díkaios* (the just), *dikaioún* (to justify), *dikaiosýnē* (justice, justification), *dikaíōma* (justification, justice, judgment), *dikaíōs* (justly), and *dikaíōsis* (justification). Taking those words into account, therefore, ask yourself a leading question: how in fact does the New Testament say we are justified? The answer of course is: by grace through faith (Eph. 2:8)—that is, by our simple trust in the graciously disreputable thing that God did when he fixed up his own insides by the death of Christ.

So Jesus ends the parable by saying, "Listen to what the unjust judge says: 'And will not God judge in favor [*poiḗsȩ ekdíkēsin,* do favorable judgment] of his own people who cry to him for help day and night? Will he not have mercy [*makrothymeí,* be bighearted] upon them?'" Pay attention to what I'm telling you, Jesus says in effect. Do you think it makes the least difference to God whether anyone's cause is just? Do you think it matters at all to him that they, even in their loss and death, still try to function like winners? I tell you, none of that amounts to a hill of beans with him. He finds all the lost whether they think they're lost or not. He raises all the dead whether they acknowledge their death or not. It's not that they have to make some heroic effort to get themselves to cooperate with him; and it's certainly not that they have to spend a lot of time praying and yammering to get him to cooperate with them. Don't you see? It's the bare fact of their lostness and death, not their interpretation of it or their acceptance of it, that cries out to him day and night. Lost sheep don't have to ask the shepherd to find them. Lost coins don't have to make long prayers to get the housewife to hunt for them. And lost sons—who may think that they are only allowed to ask for some plausible, sawed-off substitute for salvation—are always going to be totally surprised by the incredible, unasked-for party that just falls in their laps. All they have to be is lost. Not fancy lost, perceptively lost, or repentantly lost; just plain lost. And just plain dead, too. Not humbly dead, engagingly dead, or cooperatively dead; just dead. "I, if I be lifted up," Jesus says, "will draw all to me": the sheep, the coin, the son, the widow—the whole sorry lot of you. You don't have to do a blessed thing, make a single prayer, or have a legitimate case. I do it all.

Finally, though, Jesus answers the rhetorical question he proposed when he first began to point the moral of the parable of the Unjust Judge, namely: "Will not God judge in favor of his people . . . and have mercy on them?" His answer is: "You bet he will—and soon" *(en táchei)*. Forget, if you will, all the hopeless arguments over what Jesus, in his first-century Jewish mind, might have meant by the word "soon." And forget especially all the critics' assertions of what he couldn't possibly have meant. For my money, none of that matters: at the very least, he said *soon* because, for some reason unknown to us, he felt like saying *soon*. In any case, both in terms of the parable of the Unjust Judge and in terms of what Jesus rather shortly did on the cross, I opt for the crucifixion and resurrection as the most likely *scriptural* referents of that *soon*. (At the risk of having even my temporary work permit withdrawn by the New Testament Critics' Union, let me say plainly what I mean by a scriptural referent. For my money, the *scriptural* meaning of a passage is the one it has in the entire context of the biblical revelation of God, not just what it might mean in its particular time and place. And that meaning is the overarchingly important one, since it takes into account not only the licks that the Holy Spirit, the Scriptures' presiding genius, got in at the time the passage was originally composed but also all the other scriptural licks he got in before, during, and after its composition. It even includes the consummate lick of getting the church finally to agree about just which Scriptures he actually presided over.)

In any case, what Jesus actually did *soon* was die and rise—and that, for me, governs everything. Like the unjust judge, he went out of business. He issued a totally disreputable verdict of forgiveness over an entire race of unrepentant, unreconstructed nuisances just because he didn't want to be bothered with the unnecessary job of proving what they had already proved, namely, that they were a bunch of jerks. All that mattered to him was that they were *pitiful* jerks. And because he was willing to drop dead to give them a break—because, like the judge who was tired of the widow's hassling, he was tired of having his cage rattled by a worldful of idiots—he destroyed himself rather than have to destroy them. And that, Virginia, is why "There is therefore now no condemnation to those who are in Christ Jesus." There is no condemnation because there is no condemner. There is no hanging judge and there is no angry God: he has knocked himself clean off the bench and clear out of the God Union. Nobody but a bad judge could have issued a favorable judgment on our worthless cases; and nobody but a failed God—a God finally and for all out of any recognizable version of the God business—could possibly have been bighearted enough to throw a going-out-of-business sale for the likes of us.

Jesus concludes the parable, however, with a warning in the form of yet another rhetorical question. "Still," he says (*plēn:* nevertheless, notwithstanding, in spite of all the lovely good news I've just given you), "when the Son of man comes, will he find faith *[pístin]* on the earth?" The implied answer, of course, is no: a dead God is no more acceptable to a world of respectable winners than a corrupt, self-pleasing judge would be to the members of the ABA Ethics Committee. As they would not trust such a judge to sit on the bench, so we will do almost anything to avoid putting our faith in a God who doesn't come up to our standards for divinity.

And there, if you will, is the ultimate dilemma of the church.

The one thing it doesn't dare try to sell—for fear of being laughed out of town—turns out to be the only thing it was sent to sell. But because it more often than not caves in to its fear of ridicule, it gives the world the perennial spectacle of an institution eager to peddle anything but its authentic merchandise. I can stand up in the pulpit and tell people that God is angry, mean, and nasty; I can tell them he is so good they couldn't possibly come within a million miles of him; and I can lash them into a frenzy of trying to placate him with irrelevant remorse and bogus good behavior—with sacrifices and offerings and burnt offerings and sin offerings, all of which are offered by the law (Heb. 10:8); but I cannot stand there and tell them the truth that he no longer cares a fig for their sacred guilt or their precious lists of good deeds, responsible outlooks, and earnest intentions. I can never just say to them that God has abolished all those oppressive, godly requirements in order that he might grant them free acceptance by his death on the cross. Because when I do that, they can conclude only one of two things: either that I am crazy or that God is. But alas, God's sanity is the ultimate article of their non-faith. Therefore, despite Scripture's relentless piling up of proof that he is a certifiable nut—that he is the Crazy Eddie of eternity, whose prices are *insane*—it always means that I am the one who gets offered a ticket to the funny farm.

Which is all right, I guess. After the unjust steward, the unjust judge, and the God who hasn't got the integrity to come down from the cross and zap the world into shape, it's a nice, rough approximation of justification by grace alone, through faith.

CHAPTER EIGHTEEN

Death and Resurrection One Last Time

The Pharisee and the Publican

—which, in turn is exactly the right note on which to begin my finale on the parable of the Pharisee and the Publican. Since I have mentioned my suicidal tendencies as a preacher, let me offer you a full-blown example of such self-destructiveness:

An ordinary sermon on the two men who went up to the temple

Luke, chapter 18, verses 9-14: "Jesus also told this parable to some who trusted in themselves that they were righteous *[díkaioi]* and despised everybody else. Two men went up to the temple to pray: one, a Pharisee, the other, a tax collector. The Pharisee stood apart by himself and prayed thus: 'God, I thank you that I am not like others are, greedy, unjust *[ádikoi]*, adulterers—and I thank you especially that I am not like this tax collector. I fast two days every week and I give you a tenth of all my income.' But the tax collector stood a long way off and would not even raise his eyes to heaven. Instead, he beat on his breast and said, 'O God, be merciful *[hilásthēti]* to me, a sinner.' I tell you, this man went to his house justified *[dedikaiōménos]* rather than the other: for everyone who exalts himself will be humbled, but he who humbles himself will be exalted."

In the Name of the Father and of the Son and of the Holy Spirit. Amen.

Now then. The first thing to get off the table is the notion that this parable is simply a lesson in the virtue of humility. It is not. It is an instruction in the futility of religion—in the idleness of the proposition that there is anything at all you can do to put yourself right with God. It is about the folly of even trying. The parable occurs after a series of illustrations of what Jesus means by faith, and it comes shortly before he announces, for the third time, that he will die and rise again. It is therefore not a recommendation to adopt a humble religious stance rather than a proud one; rather it is a warning to drop all religious stances—and all moral and ethical ones, too—when you try to grasp your justification before God. It is, in short, an exhortation to move on to the central point of the Gospel: faith in a God who raises the dead.

Consider the characters in this parable. Forget the prejudice that Jesus' frequently stinging remarks about Pharisees have formed in your mind. Give this particular Pharisee all the credit you can. He is, after all, a good man. To begin with, he is not a crook, not a timeserver, not a womanizer. He takes nothing he hasn't honestly earned, he gives everyone he knows fair and full measure, and he is faithful to his wife, patient with his children, and steadfast for his friends. He is not at all like this publican, this tax-farmer, who is the worst kind of crook: a legal one, a big operator, a mafia-style enforcer working for the Roman government on a nifty franchise that lets him collect—from his fellow Jews, mind you, from the people whom the Romans might have trouble finding, but whose whereabouts he knows and whose language he speaks—all the money he can bleed out of them, provided only he pays the authorities an agreed flat fee. He has been living for years on the cream he has skimmed off their milk money. He is a fat cat who drives a stretch limo, drinks nothing but Chivas Regal, and never shows up at a party without at least two $500-a-night call girls in tow.

The Pharisee, however, is not only good; he is religious. And not hypocritically religious, either. His outward uprightness is matched by an inward discipline. He fasts twice a week and he puts his money where his mouth is: ten percent off the top for God. If you know where to find a dozen or two such upstanding citizens, I know several parishes that will accept delivery of them, no questions asked and all Jesus' parables to the contrary notwithstanding.

But best of all, this Pharisee thanks God for his happy state. Luke says that Jesus spoke this parable to those who trusted in themselves that they were righteous. But Jesus shows us the Pharisee in the very act of giving God the glory. Maybe the reason he went up to the temple to pray was that, earlier in the week, he slipped a little and thought of his righteousness as his own doing. Maybe he said to himself, "That's terrible, I must make a special visit to the temple and set my values straight by thanking God."

But what does Jesus tell you about this good man—about this entirely acceptable candidate for the vestry of your parish? He tells you not only that he is in bad shape, but that he is in worse shape than a tax-farmer who is as rotten as they come and who just waltzes into the temple and does nothing more than say as much. In short, he tells you an unacceptable parable.

For you would—I know I would—gladly accept the Pharisee's pledge card and welcome him to our midst. But would you accept me for long if I had my hand in the church till to the tune of a Cadillac and a couple of flashy whores? Would you (would the diocesan authorities) think it was quite enough for me to come into church on a Sunday, stare at the tips of my shoes, and say, "God be merciful to me a sinner?" Would the bishop write me a letter commending my imitation of the parable and praising me for preaching not only in word but in deed? Jesus, to be sure, says that God would; I myself, however, have some doubts about you and the bishop. You might find it a bit too . . . vivid. There seems to be just no way of dramatizing this parable from our point of view. That being the case, turn it around and look at it from God's.

God is sitting there in the temple, busy holding creation in being—thinking it all into existence, concentrating on making the hairs on your head jump out of nothing, preserving the seat of my pants, reconciling the streetwalkers in Times Square, the losers on the Bowery, the generals in the Pentagon, and all the worms under flat rocks in Brazil. And in come these two characters. The Pharisee walks straight over, pulls up a chair to God's table, and whips out a pack of cards. He fans them, bridges them, does a couple of one-handed cuts and an accordion shuffle, slides the pack over to God, and says, "Cut. I'm in the middle of a winning streak." And God looks at him with a sad smile, gently pushes the deck away, and says, "Maybe you're not. Maybe it just ran out."

So the Pharisee picks up the deck again and starts the game himself. "Acey-Ducey, okay?" And he deals God a two of fasting and a king of no adultery. And God says, "Look, I told you. Maybe this is not your game. I don't want to take your money."

"Oh, come on," says the Pharisee. "How about seven-card stud, tens wild? I've been real lucky with tens wild lately." And God looks a little annoyed and says, "Look, I meant it. Don't play me. The odds here are always on my side. Besides, you haven't even got a full deck. You'd be smarter to be like the guy over there who came in with you. He lost his cards before he got here. Why don't you both just have a drink on the house and go home?"

Do you see now what Jesus is saying in this parable? He is saying that as far as the Pharisee's ability to win a game of justification with God is concerned, he is no better off than the publican. As a matter of fact, the Pharisee is worse off; because while they're both losers, the publican at least has the sense to recognize the fact and trust God's offer of a free drink. The point of the parable is that they are both dead, and their only hope is someone who can raise the dead.

"Ah but," you say, "is there no distinction to be made? Isn't the Pharisee somehow less further along in death than the publican? Isn't there some sense in which we can give him credit for the real goodness he has?"

To which I answer, you are making the same miscalculation as the Pharisee. Death is death. Given enough room to maneuver, it eventually produces total deadness. In the case of the publican, for example, his life so far has been quite long enough to force upon him the recognition that, as far as his being able to deal with God is concerned, he is finished. The Pharisee, on the other hand, looking at his clutch of good deeds, has figured that they are more than enough to keep him in the game for the rest of his life.

But there is his error. For the rest of his life here, maybe. But what about for the length and breadth of eternity? Take you own case. Let us suppose that you are an even better person than the Pharisee. Let us assume that you are untempted to any sin except the sin of envy, and that even there, your resolve is such that, for the remainder of your days, you never do in fact fall prey to that vice. Are you so sure, however, that the robustness of your virtue is the only root of your unjealous disposition? Might not a very large source of it be nothing more than lack of opportunity? Have you never thought yourself immune to some vice only to find that you fell into it when the temptation became sufficient? The lady who resists a five-dollar proposition sometimes gives in to a five-million-dollar one: men who would never betray friends have been known to betray friends they thought were about to betray them. The reformer immune to the corruption of power finds corruption easier as he gains power.

Take your dormant envy then. From now till the hour of your death, you may very well not meet that one person who will galvanize it into action. But in eternity—in that state where there are no limits to opportunity, when you have a literal forever in which to meet, literally, everybody—is your selflessness so profound that you can confidently predict you will never be jealous of anyone? Is the armor of your humility so utterly without a chink?

There, you see, is the problem as God sees it. For him, the eternal order is a perpetual-motion machine: it can tolerate no friction at all. Even one grain of sand—one lurking vice in one of the redeemed—given long enough, will find somewhere to lodge and something to rub on. And that damaged something, given another of the infinite eternities within eternity itself, will go off center and shake the next part loose. And then the next; and so straight on into what can only be the beginning of the end: the very limitlessness of the opportunity for mischief will eventually bring the whole works to a grinding halt.

What Jesus is saying in this parable is that no human goodness is good enough to pass a test like that, and that therefore God is not about to risk it. He will not take our cluttered life, as we hold it, into eternity. He will take only the clean emptiness of our death in the power of Jesus' resurrection. He condemns the Pharisee because he takes his stand on a life God cannot use; he commends the publican because he rests his case on a death that God can use. The fact, of course, is that they are both equally dead and therefore both alike receivers of the gift of resurrection. But the trouble with the Pharisee is that for as long as he refuses to confess the first fact, he will simply be unable to believe the second. He will be justified in his death, but he will be so busy doing the bookkeeping on a life he cannot hold that he will never be able to enjoy himself. It's just misery to try to keep count of what God is no longer counting. Your entries keep disappearing.

If you now see my point, you no doubt conclude that the Pharisee is a fool. You are right. But at this point you are about to run into another danger. You probably conclude that he is also a rare breed of fool—that the number of people who would so blindly refuse to recognize such a happy issue out of all their afflictions has got to be small. There you are wrong. We all refuse to see it. Or better said, while we sometimes catch a glimpse of it, our love of justification by works is so profound that at the first opportunity we run from the strange light of grace straight back to the familiar darkness of the law.

You do not believe me? I shall prove it to you: the publican goes down to his house justified rather than the other. Well and good, you say; yes indeed. But let me follow him now in your mind's eye as he goes through the ensuing week and comes once again to the temple to pray. What is it you want to see him doing those seven days? What does your moral sense tell you he ought at least try to accomplish? Are you not itching, as his spiritual adviser, to urge him into another line of work—something perhaps a little more upright than putting the arm on his fellow countrymen for fun and profit? In short, do you not feel compelled to insist on at least a little reform?

To help you be as clear as possible about your feelings, let me set you two exercises. For the first, take him back to the temple one week later. And have him go back there with nothing in his life reformed: walk him in this week as he walked in last—after seven full days of skimming, wenching, and high-priced Scotch. Put him through the same routine: eyes down, breast smitten, God be merciful, and all that. Now then. I trust you see that on the basis of the parable as told, God will not mend his divine ways any more than the publican did his wicked ones. He will do this week exactly what he did last: God, in short, will send him down to his house justified. The question in this first exercise is, do you like that? And the answer, of course, is that you do not. You gag on the unfairness of it. The rat is getting off free.

For the second exercise, therefore, take him back to the temple with at least some reform under his belt: no wenching this week perhaps, or drinking cheaper Scotch and giving the difference to the Heart Fund. What do you think now? What is it that you want God to do with him? Question him about the extent to which he has mended his ways? For what purpose? If God didn't count the Pharisee's impressive list, why should he bother with this two-bit one? Or do you want God to look on his heart, not his list, and commend him for good intentions at least? Why? The point of the parable was that the publican confessed that he was dead, not that his heart was in the right place. *Why are you so bent on destroying the story by sending the publican back for his second visit with the Pharisee's speech in his pocket?*

The honest answer is, that while you understand the thrust of the parable with your mind, your heart has a desperate need to believe its exact opposite. And so does mine. We all long to establish our identity by seeing ourselves as approved in other people's eyes. We spend our days preening ourselves before the mirror of their opinion so we will not have to think about the nightmare of appearing before them naked and uncombed. And we hate this parable because it says plainly that it is the nightmare that is the truth of our condition. We fear the publican's acceptance because we know precisely what it means. It means that we will never be free until we are dead to the whole business of justifying ourselves. But since that business is our life, that means not until *we* are dead.

For *Jesus came to raise the dead.* Not to reform the reformable, not to improve the improvable . . . but then, I have said all that. Let us make an end: as long as you are struggling like the Pharisee to be alive in your own eyes—and to the precise degree that your struggles are for what is holy, just, and good—you will resent the apparent indifference to your pains that God shows in making the effortlessness of death the touchstone of your justification. Only when you are finally able, with the publican, to admit that you are dead will you be able to stop balking at grace.

It is, admittedly, a terrifying step, You will cry and kick and scream before you take it, because it means putting yourself out of the only game you know. For your comfort though, I can tell you three things. First, it is only one step. Second, it is not a step out of reality into nothing, but a step from fiction into fact. And third, it will make you laugh out loud at how short the trip home was: it wasn't a trip at all; you were already there.

Death—for the third and last time—is absolutely all of the resurrection we can now know. The rest is faith.

In the Name of the Father and of the Son and of the Holy Spirit. Amen.